D1097893

Designing and Making
Hats and Headpieces

Designing and Making
Hats and Headpieces

Judy Bentinck

THE CROWOOD PRESS

First published in 2014 by
The Crowood Press Ltd
Ramsbury, Marlborough
Wiltshire SN8 2HR

www.crowood.com

© Judy Bentinck 2014

All rights reserved. No part of this publication may be reproduced or transmitted in any form or
by any means, electronic or mechanical, including photocopy, recording, or any information
storage and retrieval system, without permission in writing from the publishers.

British Library Cataloguing-in-Publication Data
A catalogue record for this book is available from the British Library.

ISBN 978 1 84797 822 6

Front cover: Judy Bentinck Millinery. Style: Wool Felt Cloche. Photographer: Alistair Cowin.
Model: Tamlyn Williams. Make-up and hair: Sammy Carpenter.

Frontispiece: Judy Bentinck Millinery. Style: Ivory Bridal Fascinator.
Photographer: Alistair Cowin. Model: Tamlyn Williams. Make-up and hair: Sammy Carpenter.

Acknowledgements
Enormous thanks to Freya Berry and Tim Bentinck for their IT skills, support and understanding.
Thanks also to the milliners who have allowed me to use their photographs and to Natasha
Moorhouse for the use of her hands. Lastly, thanks to all at The Crowood Press for their patience
and to Alistair Cowin for his beautiful model shots.

Step-by step photographs by Tim and Judy Bentinck.
Diagrams by Selina Burgess.

Typeset by Sharon Dainton, Isis Design.
Printed and bound in India by Replika Press Pvt. Ltd.

Contents

Chapter 1
Introduction

Why do people wear hats? To keep the rain off, to keep warm, to be part of a team, to shield the sun from their eyes – or for no practical reason, simply to look lovely. Hats are sexy and the process of creating something that is both a sculptural work of art and an alluring, flattering adornment to a woman's outfit is sexy too, and enormously satisfying. I love it and in this book I'll show you how to do it.

Wearing a hat for style rather than just for need has been part of all cultures for thousands of years. Traditional millinery lost favour for a while in the 1960s, in the UK at least, as young people dictated fashion for the first time in history, with the flower-power rebellion and back-combed bouffant hairdos taking the place of the conventional crowning glory.

In Britain Princess Diana almost single-handedly reignited the millinery industry and, while the Queen has never stopped wearing them and Ascot has always demanded them, the wedding of Prince William and Kate Middleton certainly focused a lot of attention on hats and their wearers. Today special occasions are full of beautiful headwear – from fabulous fascinators to pretty pillboxes to colossal cartwheels!

I have always loved hats. As a child I was one of the few girls who happily wore their hat to school, come rain or shine. At college I would scour charity shops for perky titfers or huge floppy brimmed creations, and I always sported a flat cap for weekend walks.

In my early career as a costume designer and wardrobe supervisor I occasionally had to create hats but I had no real idea how to do it – I didn't know what a block was until my first millinery lesson in 2000 but that was the day I fell in love! It was so exciting to discover that millinery involved sculpture, textiles, style, colour, flair, proportion and, most of all, passion!

Today I combine running my couture millinery business with teaching. I love passing on the traditional skills that were taught to me by Rose Cory, Royal Warrant Holder, and watching the delight on the faces of my students as they experience the same excitement at this most creative of crafts. It has prompted me to write this book, to let you, the reader, discover for yourself the joy of creating something beautiful and wearable. To be inspired and excited and to open up a new world of all things hats!

LEFT: Judy Bentinck Millinery. Style: parisisal pillbox hat. Photographer: Alistair Cowin. Model: Tamlyn Williams. Make-up and hair: Sammy Carpenter.

Chapter 2
So What is Millinery?

Millinery is the term used to describe the craft of making hats and headpieces for women. The word milliner derives from the seventeenth century when Milan in Italy was the centre for the beautiful fine straws, ribbons and general haberdashery suitable to trim and create ladies' hats. Salesmen who travelled across Europe to Britain became known as 'the men from Milan' or 'Milaners', which evolved into milliners. (Men's hats on the other hand are made by a hatter. There are milliners who do both, for example the wonderful and prolific Stephen Jones has a range called Miss Jones for women and Boy Jones for men.)

There are several well known idioms about hat-making and hats in general; you may have heard of some of them but might not be aware of how they came into being. Being as 'mad as a hatter', for example, was an expression pertaining to the unfortunate side-effects of working with mercury nitrate, a chemical used most notably during the Victorian era to soften fur in the felt-making process. Although these feltmakers were known to drink copiously as a result of their dusty working conditions, it was the long-term inhalation of mercury that poisoned the hatters and produced a number of inebriate symptoms, which often developed into tremors, delirium, paralysis and eventual death. Mercury had been removed from the process in Britain by the end of the nineteenth

century but in some areas of the United States its use continued until as recently as the early 1940s. Mercury poisoning was known as the 'Danbury shakes' in the US owing to the concentration of hat-making in Danbury, Connecticut.

There are several other expressions from the times when hats were commonplace which have survived to the present and are used in everyday speech without us even thinking about the original meaning. This goes to show what an important clothing item hats always were until the decline of the hat-

making industry in the 1960s, and how, throughout the different fashions and styles of the decades, the hat remained an essential accessory. Idioms like 'keep it under your hat' (to keep a secret), 'take my hat off to you' (show respect, praise or admiration), 'to pull it out of a hat' (achieve a surprise or trick), 'at the drop of a hat' (to act quickly, instantly), 'to wear more than one hat' (having lots of jobs or responsibilities) and 'old hat' (out of date or old-fashioned) all give us a glimpse into the past. The word has also been used more recently, for

Japanese milliners celebrating St Catherine's Day.

LEFT: Judy Bentinck Millinery. Style: silk dupion-covered cocktail hat.
Photographer: Alistair Cowin. Model: Tamlyn Williams.
Make-up and hair: Sammy Carpenter.

example in the 1980s Paul Young song 'Wherever I Lay My Hat (That's My Home)', showing how significant hats really were. In fact, millinery even has its own patron saint, St Catherine, and her patronage is celebrated annually on 25 November. Originally the festival was to honour unmarried women over the age of twenty-five – known as 'Catherinettes' – where everyone would wish them a hasty end to their single status. Well-meaning friends would make the Catherinettes hats in green and yellow colours to symbolize fertility, faith and wisdom. This is, of course, outmoded these days but it still provides a welcome excuse for milliners to get together for a party! There are many other fascinating and quirky stories surrounding the hat-making industry and its rich history, and you can find out more by referring to the Further Reading section.

Components of the Hat: How it is Constructed

Hats come in all shapes and sizes. The hats featured in this book are designed to make a woman look gorgeous. If you've ever wondered how such beautiful things are actually constructed, you will find an explanation below with images to show the various parts.

Bespoke vs Mass-Produced Hats

Hats are made and sold in different ways. A hat that is created for a particular individual's outfit for a special occasion is known as a bespoke hat. Milliners who create one-offs or only produce two or three of a design are called Model Milliners. Mass-produced hats are factory made, using specialist machinery to speed up the blocking and making process, thus creating much cheaper hats and making them more accessible to a larger number of people.

COMPONENTS OF THE HAT:

- The crown consists of the tip (the top of the hat) and sideband (the sides).

- The brim is made up of the headfitting (where the crown fits the brim) and the headribbon, which is attached inside the headfitting and is made of millinery petersham. It rests against the head to ensure a comfortable and secure fit. The wire supporting the outer edge of the brim is covered by the binding, which can be made from a variety of materials.

- The trim is the finishing detail to cover the join between the brim and the crown. More trimmings can also be added, for example flowers, feathers, swirls and veiling.

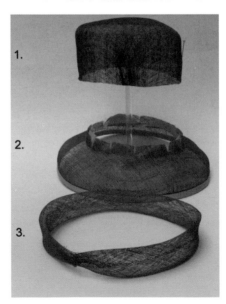

1: the crown; 2: the brim; 3: the trim.

These hats can be found in department stores and on the high street.

The vast majority of men's hats are mass produced, though the quality and cost vary widely. It is unusual for a man to have a bespoke hat made these days, although occasionally they can be commissioned for a chap with an exceptionally large or small head. It is interesting to note that women are now sporting a variety of men's styles, for example the trilby, the fedora and the bowler – an example of which is featured in this book. Interestingly both the trilby and the fedora have their origins in fictional female characters. Trilby was the main character in George du Maurier's novel of the same name, in the stage adaptation of which the leading actress wore the distinctive hat that went on to become the ever-popular trilby. Similarly, the fedora comes from a stage play featuring Sarah Bernhardt. She played Princess Fedora, a cross-dresser who wore the characteristic flat-brimmed hat with pinched front that later became popular with gangsters and was worn by Harrison Ford in the Indiana Jones movies. The beret was a traditional military hat for men, which has since been adopted as a fashion item for women. There is a beret pattern and making instructions later in this book.

Karen Henriksen Millinery. Girl Racer Collection. Style: Lombardi. Photographer: Tim Scott, Fluid Images. Models: Danni Menzies and James Pike. Make-up and hair: Polly Mann.

Keely Hunter Millinery. Shapka Collection. Styles: black fedora and red trilby.
Photographer: Peter Fingleton. Model: Anna A @ Union.

In this book you will find instructions on how to make a variety of hats. They are grouped into three sections: blocked hats, which are created on a solid shape called a block; headpieces, which are made without blocks and thus are unstructured; and hats made using fabric and patterns (*see* Chapter 8).

At the beginning of each project is a list of everything needed to make the hat. The quantities of materials are approximate, but any left-overs can be kept and used for other trims or designs in the future. There is also a list of the techniques used, and an indication of where to find more detailed explanations of both trimmings and techniques.

Millinery is an exciting and highly imaginative craft, with endless possibilities for creative flair and innovative design.

Chapter 3
Materials, Tools and Equipment

Millinery Equipment

The good news is that most of what you need to get started with your first millinery creation consists of everyday items that you probably already have in your sewing kit, tool box or around the house. There are, however, a few specialist millinery items you will need to consider investing in before you start. The most important of these are: blocks; dolly heads; stiffeners; millinery needles in sizes 7–9 (7 for strong material; 9 for fine fabrics); and millinery cotton-covered wire.

Blocks

Blocks are moulds that are used to create hats. They usually come as separate crown blocks and brim blocks, although some styles have blocks made to include both crown and brim. Traditionally, hat blocks were carved from wood by a craftsman known as a block-maker; with the resurgence in popularity of hat-wearing in recent years, the need for hat blocks for milliners and millinery students has been reignited, with vintage blocks also becoming much sought after for original period shapes. There are far more block-makers these days, some of whom are listed in the Suppliers List at the back of the book.

Older blocks tend to be made of much harder wood than the modern ones, and some people find pinning into these hardwoods difficult. Therefore it is important to learn to use a thimble effectively. If you find this hard to master, an easier way is to use red-headed purpose-made blocking pins or regular drawing pins. Many modern blocks are made from obeche wood, which is quite easy to pin into, and some

A selection of wooden blocks, courtesy of Atelier Millinery.

How a crown and brim block are placed together to form a picture hat shape.

LEFT: Selection of millinery materials at Atelier Millinery, London..

Clockwise from left: Blocking spring; elastic band (a useful alternative to a blocking spring); cling film (Saran wrap) for protecting your blocks from dust and dye; wooden dolly head; tape measure without flat end; blocking pins; string; a corset bone; crown block on stand; small block; red blocking pins; kitchen palette knife for easing hats off blocks; thimble for pushing blocking pins in; cloche brim block; and wire-cutters (useful for pulling pins out).

are now being made from balsa wood, which is a soft wood. As a general rule, try to keep your blocking pins separate from any others as these may have some residue of stiffener on them that makes them unsuitable for pinning into fabric as they will be blunter than usual.

Generally milliners start with just a few blocks, as they can be interchanged and can be very versatile. For example, a standard dome-shaped crown block can be used with a variety of brim blocks to create very different styles. Some block-makers offer multi block sets or block bundles, which are ideal for starting out. Freeform hats are made without blocks, while cut and sewn hats use paper patterns, so there is a wide choice of methods.

BLOCKING SPRINGS
A blocking spring is a very useful millinery tool. It helps you block the crown of a hat by holding the material in place as you pull and pin. It is especially useful for the 'pull down' method (see Chapter 6). It gives a much neater result

in less time and with fewer pins than if you use pins alone. Rings come in different sizes and correspond to the head size of the block you are using. You can buy blocking springs from specialist millinery suppliers such as Parkin Fabrics in Preston, UK. An alternative to a blocking spring is to use large elastic bands or a ball of ordinary (cotton) string.

Dolly Heads

A dolly or poupee head is ideal for working with hats and fascinators, as it allows you to view and shape the hat according to how it is going to be worn. It also, of course, provides the perfect stand to display your hats as well. Wooden dolly heads can be bought from specialist suppliers and come in different head sizes. Polystyrene heads as used by hairdressers and wigmakers are often a small head size but they are very inexpensive and really useful. They can be bought from shopfitters, hairdressing suppliers or online. It is possible to make your own dolly heads out of fabric-covered buckram but it is a time-consuming process.

A pull-down blocking spring in use.

A group of dolly heads.

Stiffeners

Different milliners have their own preferences for which stiffener they use, how much and when, depending on the material they're working with. Generally the water-based stiffener works best with sinamay but nowadays most sinamay comes ready stiffened, which removes the need for extra stiffener. However, spraying with water to soften the sinamay ready for blocking can sometimes wash some of this stiffener away, especially if spraying is repeated during the blocking. In this case straw stiffener can be added afterwards. All straws can be stiffened both before and after blocking using a straw stiffener, which is painted on like a varnish. Felt can be stiffened with diluted water-based stiffener or felt stiffener.

STEAMING AND STRETCHING

Professional milliners often use Jiffy hat steamers. These are bulky and expensive, but by no means essential – as an alternative you can use either a domestic kettle or a hand-held clothes steamer.

Another item often found in a milliner's studio is a hat stretcher. Again, this is a cumbersome and expensive outlay. Smaller and cheaper alternatives called hat expanders are available from specialist block-makers.

Wire

Millinery wire comes cotton-covered in either black or white. A stiffer wire, with a diameter of 1.2mm, is best for holding brims. Fine wire is good for trimmings, and a very fine wire is ideal when working with hand-made flowers or tiaras. Strong millinery wire comes in a coil 50m long. An alternative is brim wire, which is clear plastic and comes in two diameters. Some shops sell wire by the yard (metre).

Left to right: hand-held steamer; kettle; and Jiffy steamer.

Professional hat stretcher at the back, with a hat expander in the foreground.

Clockwise from left: felt stiffener; spray stiffener; straw stiffener; water-based stiffener; roll of kitchen paper; jam-jar with diluted water-based stiffener solution; and household paint brushes for applying stiffener wrapped in cling-film to keep them soft.

Left to right: Brim reed wire; flower wire; and cotton-covered millinery wire (1.2mm).

Sewing Equipment

Needles

Different materials need different-sized needles. Generally, for fine sewing, such as a silk binding, use a thin needle called a 'sharp' (these come in packs of sizes 3–9) as a thick milliner's needle would be difficult to use. For more substantial sewing tasks, such as joining the crown to the brim, use a longer, thicker millinery needle (straw/milliner's needle) as this will be stronger and firmer. Needles that are too small can be easily damaged when pushed through stiff or multi-layered fabric, so always check your needle is appropriate for the job in hand. With time and use, needles can become blunt and you will feel a resistance when sewing. This indicates you need to change needles.

Clockwise from left: Fine pins for sewing; thimbles for pinning and sewing; variety of sewing threads; pincushion (essential to avoid losing pins and needles); hand sewing needles; household pins for blocking; and long quilters' pins for holding trims in place.

Left to right: heavy steel rule which can be used with knives; disposable craft knife; Stanley knife for cutting felt, leather and fur; large everyday scissors for cutting millinery materials; wire-cutters (or pliers with a cutting edge); snips for cutting threads; unpicker; small sharp scissors for snipping and cutting into small areas; and good quality scissors for silks and fine fabrics.

Tape Measures

All tape measures stretch over time, but good quality linen tape measures last a lot longer. It's useful to have one with metric measurements on one side and imperial on the other, and be sure to get one without a 2in steel end, as this inhibits measuring around curves.

Miscellaneous Items

Cutting Tools

Ideally it is best to have different pairs of scissors for cutting different materials, so keep your everyday scissors away from fine fabrics. Conversely, don't use your good quality scissors on straw and paper as they will go blunt in no time. Scissors can be sharpened professionally or with a DIY sharpener bought from a craft shop.

Heat Tools

With the exception of the electric mini iron, which can be bought online from a specialist craft retailer, all of these are household items and easy to access.

Marking Tools

All of these items can be found in a regular sewing kit. They show the different ways of marking where you will be joining and/or sewing fabrics. It is often better to sew a tack line instead of using a chalk, particularly on a straw where the chalk can easily be rubbed off.

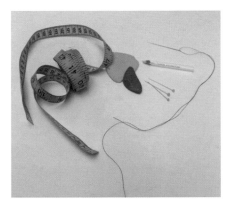

Left to right: tape measure; tailor's chalk for mark making; quilter's pins; fabric marker; needle and thread.

Household Items

A water spray is a very useful item to have to hand for softening stiffened materials. A plastic bowl is ideal for mixing water-based stiffener, and can be easily washed with boiling water and washing-up liquid.

Plastic bowl; water spray; and jug.

Useful Extras

Again, most of these can be found at home or easily purchased in your local hardware store.

Left to right: electric mini iron (useful for awkward areas and small seams); kettle (preferably with a spout but this is not essential); steam iron; dry iron (or a steam iron can be used without water); and a hairdryer (very useful to speed up drying time).

Clockwise from left: Mirror – helpful with placing trimmings and judging angles; toothbrush; suede brush; UHU glue for feathers and trims; pressing pads; Sellotape (not cheap imitations as they can't be ironed); string; baby's hair brush; pressing cloths (soft and absorbent, often used damp); nail brush; and washing-up cloth.

Fabrics

In almost all cases in millinery, when fabric has a grain we use the bias or cross (how to find the true bias is explained in Chapter 4). This means the stretchiest part of the fabric, which will curve and sit smoothly around a hat or headpiece. Natural fibres are always preferable as they iron without frazzling and creases can be removed easily.

Foundation Fabrics

These are the fabrics that aren't seen, as they are used inside the hat. Canvas and buckram are the most popular fabrics for this purpose. Buckram is treated with a starch that can be softened with water, making it very pliable. Canvas is merely wiped with a damp cloth before use. Interfacing such as stayflex and domette are used to help strengthen the hat and smooth out the texture of the foundation fabric.

Sinamay

Sinamay is a very popular hat-making material: it is lightweight, inexpensive and quite transparent. It is made of fibres from the abaca tree, which is a species of banana grown in the Philippines. It produces quite an open weave with a distinctive texture. It is woven on a loom with a warp and a weft and is bought by the yard or metre. It comes in different grades and textures and there is a huge range of commercially dyed colours.

Pinok Pok

Pinok pok is similar to sinamay but has a tighter weave and is therefore slightly less forgiving to work with. Like sinamay, pinok pok can be bought stiffened or unstiffened.

Parisisal

Other straws come in ready-made hoods called cones and capelines. Generally, the tighter the weave the more expensive it is and the harder to work with. The most frequently seen straw is parisisal. This is made from a fine, closely woven grass and is easy to block. It has a distinct grain line and a cross at the centre of the hood which is often referred to as the button. If the button sits at the centre, the grain can be controlled quite easily, unless it is a very complicated block.

Sisal

Sisal is a cheaper, more textured straw, but very versatile. All these straws take dye successfully so they can be adapted to match an outfit.

Felt

Millinery felt is produced only in cones and capelines. The flat felt you see in craft shops and the felt you can create by

Clockwise from top left: buckram; canvas; stayflex; Bondaweb; and domette.

Rolls of sinamay.

Clockwise from left: ready stiffened parisisal straw cone; natural knotted sisal capeline; open weave sisal; panama straw; parisisal flare; twisted seagrass capeline; and high quality panned parisisal capeline.

Clockwise from left: wool felt capeline; velour felt cone; and two wool felt cones.

hand are not suitable for stiffening and blocking. The felt hoods used in millinery are made from fibres from sheep's wool or rabbit/hare fur. It is a complex process that bonds the fibres together so that the hood is very strong indeed. A sheep wool felt is inexpensive and has no pile. Longer-haired felts such as peachbloom, velour and suedes have a velvet-looking pile, whereas the longest-haired felt is Melusine. Felts are often printed with animal markings and have been very popular over the last few years, but they are surprisingly expensive.

Millinery Petersham

This is a grosgrain ribbon, a cotton and viscose mix with a distinctive weave. It is predominantly cotton, which is why it is used in millinery because it can be shrunk and/or manipulated to form curves either around the hat, inside or out, as a binding or for creative trimming shapes. Do not confuse this with polyester petersham, which isn't versatile in this way. Petersham comes in a range of colours and sizes (widths) but the most widely used is no. 5, which is 1in (2.5cm) wide.

Rolls of assorted millinery petersham.

Linings

Lining a hat can be a preferred option because it gives a beautiful finish, but in some cases it is essential, for example when you are making a hat with a foundation fabric. Linings can be bought ready-made but come as a standard size so are not suitable for all shapes and sizes of hat. Chapter 6 shows you how to make your own lining for the silk dupion-covered cocktail hat.

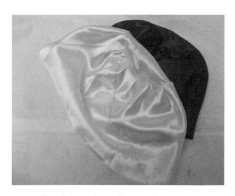

Ready-made polyester linings.

Hair Accessories

Depending on the wearer's hair length and style, there are various ways of helping to secure a hat or headpiece to the head. Combs can be fitted inside a cocktail hat or on the base of a headpiece, and come in different sizes and colours to match the hair. Ready-made fascinator bases can be bought with combs attached. Hat elastic is also useful and is worn under the hair around the back of the head to keep a hat or headpiece in place. Headbands can be a good choice for people with very fine hair, and wide headbands are great for holding substantial fascinators in place.

Clockwise: Narrow metal headband; wide and narrow satin headbands; wide and narrow velvet headbands; assorted hair combs; ivory stitched straw ready-made fascinator base; sinamay ready-made fascinator base; and small stitched straw ready-made fascinator base.

Chapter 4
Techniques

This chapter illustrates the most useful techniques that you need to create a whole variety of different hat styles and shapes. Some of the stitches may already be familiar to you if you have some experience in needlecraft or dressmaking but don't worry if they're not; with practice you will become more confident and accomplished. The other techniques explained here will enable you to make up headribbons, bindings and trimmings by ironing, curving and folding your fabrics. These stitching, shaping and sewing techniques are the essential basis for all your millinery creations.

Professional Tips

Thimbles

It is best to have a closed-end thimble (unlike the open-ended tailor's one), and to buy the right size so that it fits comfortably. Wear it on the middle finger of the hand you use to sew with. Thimbles can take a while to get used to but are essential for pushing pins into a block and for pushing the needle through layers of materials. Metal ones are preferable to plastic ones, as they are stronger and last longer.

Finishing Stitch

A number of stitches will be explained to you but for all of them a really useful tip

is how to stop your sewing coming undone. To lock the stitch firmly, sew back over the last stitch a couple of times and then pass your needle through the last loop, thus creating a knot. Then pull and cut the excess off. This will make sure your sewing doesn't unravel.

Threads

There is a variety of sewing threads to choose from but for the best quality use 100% Polyester All Purpose. It should be cut to about 22in (56cm) long, which is similar to the length tailors use when sewing; any longer and it will tangle.

In all the examples illustrated here a different coloured thread has been used so the stitches can be seen clearly. Normally a matching thread is used.

Finding the True Bias

We use the bias or cross grain in millinery because it is the stretchiest part of the material and can be curved, blocked, draped and shaped much more successfully than the straight grain.

Generally material is bought by the metre and has a 'weft', a 'warp' and a 'selvedge'. The warp is the vertical structure of the material and the weft is the horizontal weave that goes across it from left to right (a good way to

remember is that 'weft' rhymes with 'left'). The selvedge is the edge of the material where the weft has turned to create the next line of weave. It is present on both sides. It is important to note that, for millinery purposes, it doesn't stretch and needs to be removed.

Rectangle of sinamay with selvedge at the bottom, showing the straight grain with a blue dot indicating the right-hand corner.

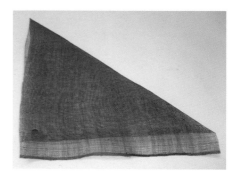

Take the right-hand corner and fold it over to create a 45 degree angle.

LEFT: Judy Bentinck Millinery. Style: felt fascinator.
Photographer: Alistair Cowin. Model: Tamlyn Williams.
Make-up and hair: Sammy Carpenter.

To find the true bias, take the top right-hand corner of your material and fold it to create a 45 degree angle at bottom right. The resulting diagonal line is the true bias or cross. The grain is the direction of the warp and weft. The cross or bias is where the warp and weft look like an X.

Stretching sinamay left to right on the diagonal.

Turn the sinamay around and stretch left to right again.

Pull the sinamay back into its original shape.

When using sinamay as a binding or as a trim, you should first stretch the sinamay in both directions on the diagonal to soften it, but make sure you put it back into its original shape before you start folding and ironing. *See also* Sinamay Binding later in this chapter.

CREATE A BIAS STRIP
There are two ways to create a bias strip. The first method is to cut along the folded line created when making the 45 degree angle and then measure your desired width from the cut edge. Alternatively you can use the fold and measure half the amount for your width.

JOINING BIAS STRIPS
This technique is used to join strips together to create a longer length of material to be used for bindings. Start by cutting two bias strips the same width; you will be sewing a seam on the straight grain. Overlay the top edges to create a V shape as illustrated, with the points extending beyond the other strip, and pin in place; then machine stitch. Once sewn, lift one strip up and lay it flat, open the seam and iron, making sure the grains match if you are using sinamay. Lastly, trim the points off. Done accurately in sinamay, this can produce an almost invisible seam and the result will be a longer length of material. This technique can also be used with strips of fabric. When using parisisal or other straws, join with a straight vertical seam as in dressmaking.

1. Pin and sew along the straight grain.

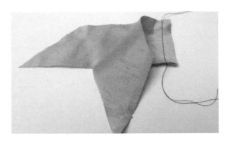

2. When opened, this produces a perfect join.

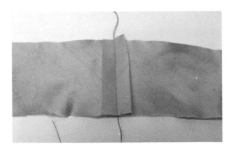

3. Joining with a vertical seam.

4. Press the seam open.

5. The finished seam.

Stitches

The first of the techniques you need is stitching. The eight stitches shown here are the most commonly used in millinery, and will be invaluable in turning your designs into reality. With any stitch that you are unfamiliar with, the best way to perfect your technique is to practise until you feel comfortable. Do remember always to keep your off-cuts because they can be used for samples and also to create new and interesting trimmings in the future.

Tacking

The simplest stitch in hand sewing is called tacking (or 'basting' in the US). It is a temporary stitch which either marks fabric or holds it together in preparation for the next step. For example, tacking might be used to hold a petersham binding in place until it is sewn with the finished stab stitch. It can also be very useful to use a tacking line instead of pins to mark where you're going to sew. It is easier to use a contrasting thread so it can be seen clearly for its purpose and for easy removal.

Using a single thread without a knot at the end, insert the needle and thread into the material and pull the cotton through, leaving about 2in (5cm) hanging on the other side so that there is no danger it will pull through and make the stitching come undone. The stitches

Example of tacking (basting). A temporary stitch.

should be regular, evenly spaced and of an equal size (approx 0.5in/1.5cm).

Running/Gathering

This is very similar to tacking but we start with a knot in the thread so that it can't come undone and the size of the stitch can vary according to its use. Its purpose is either simply to join fabric together or to gather fabric up, reducing the length and creating a ruffled effect. For an example of this technique in practice, *see* Chapter 9, the boat flower. A different version can be found in the lining of the silk dupion-covered cocktail hat. The stitch size varies according to the weight or thickness of the fabric, or how ruffled you'd like it.

1. Running stitch, sewing in and out evenly with a knot at the end.

2. Silk dupion gathered up.

Stab Stitch

This tiny stitch is used to sew a petersham headribbon in place inside the hat. The aim is to make the ribbon secure so it can't be pulled out of place

and the stitch so small it can hardly be seen. To make this stitch both neat and strong, use a single thread, as close a match in colour as possible, and sew on the very edge of the petersham next to the hat. The tiny stab is in fact a backstitch and should be the size of the groove or ridge of the petersham, the next stitch coming up two or three grooves along.

This stitch is also used when attaching a petersham binding to a wired brim or base, except the needle is angled between each stitch so it appears diagonal and the stitches are further apart than in the previous method. This speeds up the sewing considerably.

There are three different stitches that can be used to attach wire to a hat or headpiece:

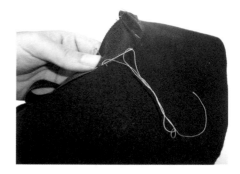
Stab stitch: a tiny backstitch.

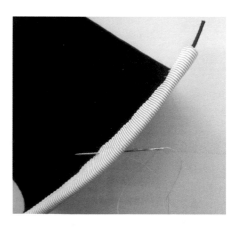
Using stab stitch, angling the needle.

Wire Stitch

This is a firm holding stitch. The thread is inserted through the loop from the back so the stitch is locked in place with a small knot on the top. Although very firm, it can show through delicate bindings.

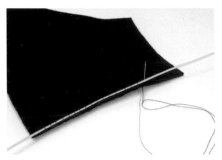

Wire stitch: inserting the needle through the loop from the back.

Wire stitch: locking the stitch in place with a knot on the top.

Quick Wire Stitch

This is a quick and easily learnt way of attaching a wire to a brim or a headpiece base. Using a single matching thread with a knot at the end, start just beyond the wire join and sew two straight stitches over the wire to make it firm, or three if it is still a bit loose. Then push the needle through from the back about 0.5in (1cm) along and sew another straight stitch. The thread has made a sloping stitch in between. The way to remember is straight, diagonal, straight and so on.

Quick wire stitch showing the straight stitch followed by the diagonal stitch.

Blanket Stitch

This is a standard dressmaking stitch where you thread the needle through the loop you have made and then pull and repeat. For some milliners this is their preferred wire stitch.

Blanket stitch: insert the needle through the loop.

Backstitch

This large stitch is used on all styles of hat to join the crown to the brim. Using double thread with a knot at the end, start at the centre back and sew forwards 1in (2.5cm), then come back through the material halfway and repeat. Pull firmly. This is a really important stitch, as it keeps the whole hat together. It creates a continuous straight line around the crown of the hat which is then covered with a band and decoration.

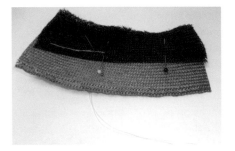

The long back stitch pictured from the front.

The long back stitch on the reverse side.

Slip Stitch

This is used to hold a sinamay, straw or fabric binding in place. It slips from the inside of the binding to the other side, running the thread along the fold line but not coming out to be seen on the outside.

On a fabric binding this stitch is used to sew on the binding invisibly. Insert the needle with a knot at the end of the

Slip stitch: running the needle along the crease of the fabric.

thread, slipping the needle into the crease of the folded part of the binding fabric. Make a stitch about half a centimetre long along the crease, being careful that it is not visible on the outside. Then push the needle through to the other side of the brim and repeat the stitch on the other side of the binding. This sewing will be invisible because the thread lies inside the fabric fold of the binding.

Oversewing

In millinery this stitch is used to create the looped headribbon. This is a very easy stitch; you simply sew over the two folded edges of petersham ribbon. With a knot at the end of a single thread, insert the needle at one end of the fold in the petersham. Push the needle through all four layers of petersham as close to the folded edge as you can, making sure you can see the stitch on the other side when opened out. Continue this tiny, shallow stitch to the other end and finish off securely. It is easier if this stitch is at a slight slope.

Oversewing at a slight angle.

Tie Tacks

This stitch is really useful for attaching trim details or feathers to a hat or headpiece. It can be used to stitch at strategic points rather than having a continuous row of stitching.

Coming in from the top (i.e. outside

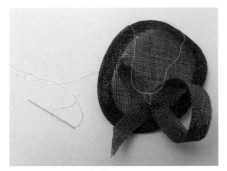

Tie tacks: knot three times to make it secure.

the crown or brim), insert a threaded needle through the hat material, leaving 3in (7.5cm) not pulled through, without a knot at the end. Sew a double stitch and then tie the two threads together to create a knot, and repeat twice more. This makes the stitch really strong. Cut the threads just above the knot.

Taking a Head Measurement

Often a hat is deemed not to suit a person but it may be that it simply doesn't fit. The one significant measurement that needs to be taken when a hat is being made to fit an individual is called the head measurement; it is referred to often in this book and is illustrated below. Place the tape measure around the widest part of the head, across the forehead and around the bump at the back of the head. It should rest comfortably with a

Measuring the widest part of the head.

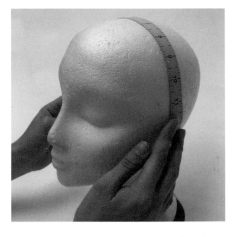

Measuring over the top of the head.

little ease. This can be achieved by slipping your finger between the tape measure and the head. A second measurement, from the top of one ear to the top of the other over the top of the head, helps to determine whether the head is wide or narrow.

Making up and Putting in a Headribbon

Millinery petersham is always used to make the headribbon. There are two ways of making up and putting in a headribbon. The technique used by couture milliners is to join the ribbon with a centre back seam and then sew it into the headfitting using very small stitches. Having taken your head measurement, cut the required length and fold the ribbon so that the two cut ends meet. Pin 1in (2.5cm) from the ends of the folded ribbon.

Next, turn both ends down and oversew with tiny stitches. Don't sew too deeply as this will create a ridge; it should lay smooth and flat when opened. This is your centre back (CB) seam.

Take your petersham CB seam and pin into place at the CB mark on your hat brim with long sharp pins placed lengthways towards the top edge of the ribbon, so pointing away from where

1. Pin 1in (2.5cm) from the cut ends.

2. When pinned, fold the ends back.

3. Sew with a small oversew stitch.

4. Hand sewn centre back seam.

5. Pin the headribbon in with long pins.

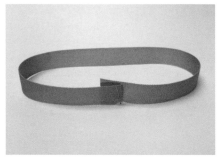

6. A simple way of making the join of your headribbon.

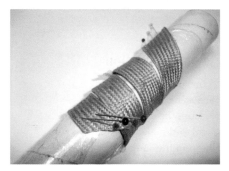

7. Wrapping the parisisal around a cardboard tube.

8. The resulting curl.

you will sew.

Hold the brim sideways so the brim is supported on your arm. Sew with stab stitch. The alternative to this technique is to curve the petersham with a hot iron, sew it into the headfitting and then simply fold back the raw edge and attach at the base, leaving the seam open. 63

Curving Parisisal

In this book we have used this technique for the trimmings on the parisisal pillbox hat, but you could also use it to create freeform styles and curved brims, as it's a versatile technique that can be used in lots of creative ways. Spray the parisisal with cold water and use a dry iron to fold in the cut top and bottom edges and then curve into the required shape by

manipulating as you go or by wrapping around a cardboard tube.

Felt

Felt can be used unstiffened by heating the hood with a wet cloth and a hot iron. This method 'felts' the hood a little more, giving it strength to hold the shape. (An example of this can be found in Chapter 9 where the felt fascinator has leaf trims treated in this way.) Otherwise a felt stiffener is painted on the inside of the hood and left to dry before steaming and blocking. The stiffener can also be applied after blocking. It must be thoroughly dry though, because white marks may appear if it is not. The wool felt cloche in Chapter 6 has the stiffener applied before steaming.

Bindings

Petersham Bindings

To bind the brim of a hat or a headpiece base as a couture milliner would, measure the circumference, add 2in (5cm) and make up your petersham into a loop in the same way as you make up the headribbon.

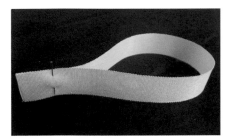

Making up a petersham loop.

If it is a large hat, please note that this can be a big measurement and accuracy is important. Place this seam at the centre back (CB) and fold the petersham lengthways over the wired edge of the brim so that it covers both sides equally. Pin all the way around by stabbing the pins vertically through the brim. Using this pinning technique is important because the regular way of using pins can distort the shape. Next, tack along the petersham using a contrasting thread so it is easy to see. The petersham may look bumpy but don't be concerned; the next step will smooth it out. Dampen a soft absorbent cloth and

Tacked on petersham, shrunk to fit.

wipe this around the petersham so the dampness is evenly distributed. The bumps will disappear and the petersham will shrink to a perfect fit.

When it is dry, sew in place with slip stitch in matching thread as close to the edge as possible. Petersham bindings have been made in this way in the wool felt cloche and the ivory bridal fascinator.

An alternative method is to curve the petersham first by folding it in half lengthways and ironing with a steam iron, curving with the other hand as you move the iron along the length. The petersham will be a little shiny as a result. Pin in place and fold the end over to create the CB seam.

Ironing folded petersham.

Sinamay Binding

A sinamay binding is a bias strip of sinamay folded in so there are no cut edges showing. It can then be shaped around a brim or a wire. Using a sinamay binding on a sinamay hat is known as a self bind. Always make sure that you stretch your sinamay both ways before beginning a binding to soften it and make sure it doesn't become narrower when you ease it around your wire. When binding, ideally one strip

Sinamay binding, as shown in the sinamay picture hat.

should be used so that there is only one resulting join. To cut the right bias strip for your binding, measure the outside of the edge to be bound and make sure you have this length, plus an overlap for the join. For an example of a sinamay binding *see* the sinamay picture hat in Chapter 6.

Fabric Binding

Making a binding from a dress-making fabric rather than a millinery material gives a softer and more luxurious finish. For more information on this, *see* the felt fascinator in Chapter 7.

An example of silk dupion fabric binding on felt.

Wire

Springing the Wire

When you buy a coil of wire, it is important not to undo all the ties. Keep one intact at all times. Push the wire out through the tie so you can measure and cut your required length. If the measurement is quite long, it is helpful to drop the coil to the floor, as its weight helps to control the springiness of the wire, making it much easier to measure and cut. The cut piece needs to have the spring taken out of it, so that it doesn't twist while you work with it. Run your thumb and forefinger over the curved wire, straightening it out. Then, to create a curve, run the padded part of your thumb along the underside of the wire and it will form a smooth curve. Be sure to eliminate any bumps or kinks in the wire before sewing in place.

Joining the Wire

When using wire to create a firm edge, you need to join it with an overlap. First, create the correct measurement with an overlap on either side, and tape at the centre point to join the wire into a loop. When you're satisfied with your measurement, use Sellotape to secure both cut ends. It is best to buy the real thing as most of the alternative tapes available can't be ironed without melting.

Join the wire with Sellotape and also tape the overlapping ends.

Pull-Down Method

This describes blocking a crown or a brim block using squares of sinamay. The material is 'pulled' over the block and pinned in a way that creates the shape but leaves creases on the bias areas. The straight grain lies flat. The creases are reduced as much as possible by pulling evenly but some will remain and will need to be covered with trimming. This method is described fully in the sinamay picture hat.

Taking your three squares of sinamay, pull down over the block.

Reduce creases by pinning and wrapping string around the block.

Judy Bentinck Millinery. Style: turquoise sinamay fascinator. Photographer: Alistair Cowin. Model: Tamlyn Williams. Make-up and hair: Sammy Carpenter.

Chapter 5
Design

Choosing and Wearing Hats

When you decide to buy a hat, what do you want it to do? Do you want to turn heads, stand out in a crowd, look elegant and stylish, be unobtrusive, or finish off the look of an outfit? Is it for a particular occasion – perhaps a wedding, the races, a christening, a garden party – or just for fun? Whatever the answer, a hat needs to fit well. You don't want to be holding on to it or pushing it out of your eyes all day. It is important to feel comfortable and confident in a hat, so choose one that suits you rather than be led by the dictates of fashion. Anyone can wear a hat, it just has to be the right one.

Face Shapes

Some say that the world is divided into two face shapes: the Horse and the Currant Bun – that is, long or round. It is an amusing thought, but it is also something of an over-simplification, because there is actually a huge variety of facial types to consider.

Faces can be oval, round, long, narrow, square, heart-shaped, high cheek-boned, thin or chubby. They can feature a small chin, a big chin, close-set eyes, wide-set eyes, big eyes, piggy eyes, a big nose, a snub nose, an aquiline nose, thin lips, full lips, a dour expression, a smiley expression and so on. And then there is hair to consider: thick, fine, curly, wavy, straight, sleek, frizzy, neat, unkempt and so on. It is also

very important to take proportion into account. Is the wearer tall and willowy or short and stout? Length of neck, width of body size and shape of face and features all need to be taken into consideration.

When dealing with hat design there are aspects of head size and face shape that need to be taken into account but, unless the design is bespoke, the wearer needs to find a hat that is right for them. It is common for people to say that they

can't wear hats because hats don't suit them. This is probably because they are either wearing the wrong hat, or they're wearing it at the wrong angle, usually on the back of the head or pulled forward over the mid brow. Very few hats are designed to be worn this way. A bespoke hat is designed and created to make one specific person look their very best.

Face shapes.

LEFT: Judy Bentinck Millinery. Style: crin headpiece.
Photographer: Alistair Cowin. Model: Tamlyn Williams.
Make-up and hair: Sammy Carpenter.

OVAL
Wear the hat straight across your brow, not on the back of your head. The crown should not be narrower than the cheekbones (this applies to all face shapes). People with an oval face shape are in luck – they can wear almost any hat style.

ROUND
Avoid cloche- or flowerpot-shaped hats and wear brims at an angle. Asymmetrical lines are good for this face shape.

SQUARE
Wear asymmetrical or tilted hats and floppy big brims. Try adding drop earrings for balance.

RECTANGLE
Don't wear crowns that are too high, so as not to elongate the face further.

OBLONG
As for rectangle, avoid tall narrow hats and try adding stud earrings to widen the face.

DIAMOND
A fedora is perfect for showcasing the cheekbones of this angular face.

INVERTED TRIANGLE
Big floppy brims worn at an angle will help to balance the proportions.

HEART
A cloche hat is perfect for this shape but be sure to avoid brims that are too small.

TRIANGLE
Balance the jaw line by having a large or sweeping brim.

GLASSES WEARERS
A brim that is turned-up or sweeping to one side can be most flattering.

Professional Design Tips

There are a few design rules applicable to hats. Of course, rules are there to be broken – and often are – but it's a good starting point. Headpieces, fascinators and cocktail hats should be worn angled over the right eye to give a chic and stylish look. If this kind of headwear is worn centrally it can look plonked and schoolgirlish and is basically unflattering. This is a key aspect of design: all headwear should be created to flatter, enhance, decorate, become and even exalt the wearer, like jewellery or any other accessory that goes beyond the merely functional.

For ladies' hats, either with or without a brim, the detail, known as the 'trim', is generally placed in one of three areas of the hat: centre front, centre back or on the right-hand side of the hat. The detail on the right can be in the middle or further forward (the trim is on the left for men). The trim must embellish the style of the hat and look good from all angles. After all, it is a three-dimensional design so it has to balance and be in harmony with the rest of the hat.

The hat has to suit the wearer, be in proportion and compliment their colouring without shouting or dominating. It is there to perfect the outfit and the person, not to overwhelm them. A general rule of thumb is that a hat should not be wider than the shoulders and hips of the wearer.

Tips for Creating Bespoke Pieces

For someone just starting out in millinery, the main concern will be learning the techniques and how it all stays together on the head. For all milliners, amateur or professional, there are other considerations to take into account, especially if the piece is a bespoke creation for an individual.

A professional milliner will always start the bespoke process with a consultation. This is their chance to ask all the relevant questions about the occasion and make sure that the hat ticks all the right boxes. Questions should include: What kind of event is it? Is the wearer a guest or do they have a significant role? What outfit will they be wearing? Do they want to be photographed in the hat? What is the venue? What time of year is it? What is the weather expected to be like? Is the location abroad? Will they need to travel with the hat? Will they be dancing in the evening? The answers can make all the difference as to how the milliner approaches the bespoke aspect of the design.

Generally, a winter hat will be made of felt and a summer one of straw, and whether the hat is likely to be exposed to the elements or not will also have implications for the design. To withstand the wind, some hat designs can be secured with combs sewn inside or with elastic that tucks under the back of the hair. If rain is expected, the wearer should be sure to have an umbrella as occasion hats generally don't like damp weather. A very important tip with regard to photography is to remember that a hat with a large brim can cast shadows over the face, so if the wearer is playing a significant role at an event and wants a hat with a big brim, choose an upturned design to avoid the shadow problem (*see*, for example, the sinamay picture hat).

The most extreme designs can be worn at an event such as Royal Ascot, whereas at a wedding you need to respect the fact that the bride should be the centre of attention. A key piece of information for determining the size of a hat is whether there will be travel involved. Creating a hat of huge dimensions might make for a spectacular effect, but it may be unwelcome if the wearer has to pay for excess baggage on their flight.

Travelling by car with a large hat is straightforward if the hat is kept in its box until arrival, otherwise the wearer may be obliged to sit at an awkward angle to fit it in. These points must be considered in the commissioning of an outrageous design.

Elements of Design

Certain elements of design are present within every project, whether you are aware of it or not. They are like the building blocks we use to create any work of art. Some of them are listed below:

Line and Direction refer to how the eye moves around the hat. This is influenced by the angle of the hat itself and any prominent feature, for example the swoop of a quill highlighting the overall shape.

Shape is the structure and essence of the hat. The easiest way to grasp this idea is to imagine the finished hat in silhouette; is each addition to the hat enhancing or detracting from the final look?

Size is an essential component of a hat. The hat has to be wearable, so the event or occasion for which it is being designed will be a factor in determining the dimensions. For example, will it fit through a doorway? Can it be worn comfortably in a car? Will it eclipse the rest of the party or block a view for others?

Texture is enormously important as the material used to make a hat fundamentally changes its nature – silk, straw or felt are totally different building blocks.

Colour is of course very important because not only should it work with the outfit, it should also complement your skin tone and hair colouring.

Contrast can add interest and dramatic effect and is also an element of many classic hats, for example cream and navy, or black and white.

Tone. A hat can influence a person's mood or the look of an outfit, sum up an occasion or define the wearer's style. A hat can be designed to be frivolous, sexy, formal, fun, elegant, playful, religious, unifying, grand, regal, attention-seeking or functional.

Pages of inspiring ideas.

Balance. In simple practical terms a hat has to have balance so that it stays on the wearer's head. In terms of design, too much emphasis on one feature will spoil the harmony of the whole.

Repetition can be an effective design feature, especially when it is used with trims. Having groups of the same flowers or feathers together adds interest and delights the eye, whilst an eye-catching trim echoing an element of the texture, pattern or colour of the main part of the hat can enhance the design.

Dominance may refer to the overall look or style of the hat, for example a trilby or a boater makes a very distinct statement, whereas a small fascinator is more about the details and the trim accessorizing the wearer's outfit, rather than being the main feature. Dominance can also refer to individual features of a hat; for example, three large flowers will be more dominant than a small birdcage veiling.

Design Inspiration

Inspiration for your designs is all around you: in nature, science, architecture, astronomy, mythology or biology. Professional designers in all disciplines often keep a scrapbook, wall chart or studio full of images from all these sources and regularly research and add to their material in order to keep their ideas fresh. Find whatever interests or excites you and investigate it, or quite simply take an idea you have seen and interpret it, making it your own. Most designers work with sketchbooks and mood boards while creating a collection and many ideas can be jotted down around a theme and then honed into a cohesive group of workable shapes, colours and directions.

For example, perhaps while scuba diving on holiday you take some photos of the coral that you encounter under the water. The colours, shapes and textures of the different species of coral inspire you and on your return home you decide to research it further. You collect more images from books and magazines, and perhaps attend an aquarium or a museum which helps you create a sketchbook or mood board for your inspiration. From here you make a design that could be a workable idea for a headpiece or hat, researching the materials that complement the original idea and add to the overall effect with trimming and finishing touches. The final piece or collection may only have a hint of the original idea – for example a key colour, shape or texture – but your design process will give it a raison d'être, cohesion and integrity.

OBSERVATION

Like drawing, observation plays a key part in making a hat, particularly when applying the ideas outlined above. It is important to try the hat on regularly (in bespoke millinery, where you are making a hat for a specific person, this is referred to as a fitting) because the angle at which the hat will eventually be worn can influence how you balance it during the designing and making stages. As different hat positions suit different face shapes, tailoring your design to the angle that best suits your wearer will ensure the best possible result.

A basic use of observation is to work using a mirror and check what the hat looks like from all angles, making sure that there isn't too much dominance in one direction, that there is balance and that the hat looks attractive and unified – and most of all suits the wearer.

Another way of ensuring this is to put the hat on a dolly (or poupee) where you can work at it from all sides and adjust the shape or trimming before you make the final decisions and sew in place.

Checking for balance on the dolly or poupee. Featuring peacock sword feathers mounted on a sinamay headband. Judy Bentinck Millinery, Corona Collection.

Chapter 6
Blocked Hats

Have you ever wondered, when browsing in a store's hat department, admiring the racegoers on Ladies Day, or watching a wedding photographer squeeze everyone into a group photo, exactly how all those hats were formed and how they hold their shape? The answer is that they are blocked. What blocks are and why they are used is covered in Chapter 3, but *essentially blocking means moulding stiffened material over a solid shape. When it dries, the well-formed structure will continue to hold that shape with the aid of wiring. Blocking is specifically a millinery technique and makes millinery distinct from other crafts, such as dressmaking.*

This chapter illustrates five different blocked hats made from a range of different materials. Each has different suggestions for trimming ideas but all are suitable for special occasions. The colour choices are, of course, yours for each hat and the trimmings can be changed; these are merely examples of ideas to stimulate and excite you.

Parisisal pillbox hat.

Wool felt cloche.

LEFT: Judy Bentinck Millinery. Style: sinamay picture hat. Photographer: Alistair Cowin. Model: Tamlyn Williams. Make-up and hair: Sammy Carpenter.

Knotted sisal and pinok pok bowler hat.

Silk dupion-covered cocktail hat.

Parisisal Pillbox Hat

Pillbox hats were originally worn as British military headgear and were sometimes also known as the Kilmarnock hat. They were worn by the Gurkha regiment, amongst others. The pillbox has a flat crown and short straight sides. This style was made iconic in the 1960s when it was favoured by Jackie Kennedy, with many different versions designed for her by Halston, the great American dress designer. The style later became known as the 'Jackie O' after she married Aristotle Onassis, and was always worn on the back of her head. Another claim to fame for the pillbox was Bob Dylan's song 'Leopardskin Pillbox Hat', which he wrote for his album *Blonde on Blonde* in 1966.

Since then the pillbox has always been a popular style as it is easy to wear, particularly as it has no brim and therefore doesn't intrude when people are greeting and embracing one another at events such as weddings. It can be worn in different positions on the head depending on the wearer's preference, and a fashionable look is to wear it at an angle over one eye. This particular pillbox hat is worn slightly to one side of the head to show more of the trim and veiling.

Parisisal pillbox hat.

FOR THIS HAT YOU WILL NEED:

A parisisal cone
Needle and thread
Scissors
Straw stiffener and brush
Pins
String
Block
Cling film (Saran wrap)
Millinery petersham
3 yards (2m) spotted veiling
2 black quills

Take the parisisal cone, spray evenly with water and leave to soften for a few minutes. Next take your block (in this case the block is the same as for the crown of the wool felt cloche) and cover it with clean cling film.

Pull the cone over the block. Parisisal cones and capelines have a cross or 'button' at the centre. This needs to be carefully lined up with the centre of the tip of the crown. It should look like an ✕ front to back. The lines of the weave will then sit parallel all the way down the hat.

The pillbox need not be very deep but pin far enough down the block to allow for a turning where the headribbon will be sewn. Pin so the straw fits firmly and as evenly as possible, pinning around

ESSENTIAL SKILLS:

For this hat it may be useful to refer to Chapter 4 for information on the headribbon and stab stitch, and to Chapter 9 for the veiling and parisisal twirls.

1. Crown block at the ready.

2. Line up your parisisal cone centrally.

3. Block your cone evenly and smoothly.

4. Once dry, paint with stiffener.

5. Iron with a piece of spare sinamay.

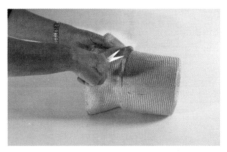

6. Once you've decided on the desired depth of your hat, cut it with scissors.

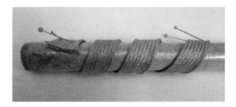

9. Curve your parisisal round a cardboard tube and remove when dry.

8. Turn the headribbon inside the hat and trim away excess parisisal.

7. Pin the headribbon at centre back (CB) and sew.

the block to ensure it is pulled tight. Wrapping a string around the lower part of the straw will help to keep it flat. Once pinned, leave to dry.

When it is completely dry, paint the blocked straw with straw stiffener, working it in thoroughly.

Once the stiffener is dry, iron with a piece of spare sinamay between the iron and the parisisal to prevent any unwanted marks being accidentally transferred.

Remove the pins and the string, tuck the palette knife inside the straw and run it around to release. Next mark the centre back (CB) and take the parisisal off the block. Now decide how deep the hat should be, remembering that if it is very shallow it won't sit comfortably on the head and must perch on the side instead. The hat in this example is 4in (10cm) deep, plus 2in (5cm) for the headfitting and turning.

Next make up the petersham headribbon; refer to Chapter 4 to see how this is done. Once you have your headribbon, start pinning it in at the CB and then sew it in using stab stitch.

Having sewn the headribbon to the straw, turn it inside so that the ribbon cannot be seen. Carefully cut away the excess straw so none can be seen beyond the headribbon. You now have a basic pillbox hat, ready to be trimmed.

The trim is made of the same parisisal as the hat and features black spot veiling. The veiling is attached first in the centre around the 'button'. The folded and curled parisisal detail is then sewn on top to hide the ends of the veiling. Glue two black quills together and sew to the hat under the twirl. Instructions on full-face veiling and parisisal twirls are given in Chapter 9. This choice of trimmings can produce a very chic and special occasion hat, but alternatively it could be trimmed with a simpler design for more everyday wear.

Here are some more inspiring ideas for pillbox-style hats; remember that pillbox blocks come in different sizes, giving you freedom to add your own creative flair.

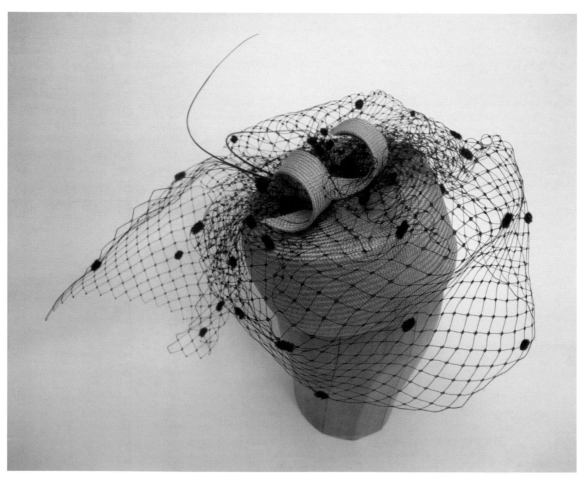

The finished hat with veiling and twirl.

Tracy Chaplin Millinery. Style: pink felt deco.
Photographer: Amanda Jobson.

Judy Bentinck Millinery. Lorelei Collection. Style: parisisal pillbox overlaid with
coque feathers and navy veiling. Photographer: Alistair Cowin.
Model: Emily Healey.

Judy Bentinck
Millinery. Portia
Collection. Style: mini
pillbox with Lady
Amherst Feathers.
Photographer: Alistair
Cowin. Model: Lucy
Shropshall.

Judy Bentinck Millinery.
Coco Rococo
Collection. Style: lilac
parisisal pillbox with
large feather spray.
Photographer: Alistair
Cowin. Model: Amy
Macdonald. Make-up
and hair: Clare Harmer.

Sinamay Picture Hat

'Picture hat' is a generic term for a big hat with a wide brim, often highly decorated with flowers, feathers and plumes. The best examples can be seen in paintings by the eighteenth-century English painter Thomas Gainsborough.

The sinamay hat shown here is created using two wooden blocks and a simple sinamay trim. Any number of other trimmings could be used, including handmade or shop-bought flowers, large ostrich feathers or buttons, bows or ribbons – the choice is vast. The essential consideration must be to keep the hat balanced and light enough to wear. In the eighteenth century these picture hats were worn on top of a substantial wig and often at quite acute angles, made possible using several long large hatpins pushed deeply into the wig. Nowadays a large picture hat should have a comfortable crown with a good fit to the head.

The simplest version of this style is the sunhat, the wide brim shading the wearer from the harsh rays of the sun but with little or no trim. The classic sunhat look of the 1930s was both chic and practical.

Sinamay is a very versatile and malleable material made from abaca or banana fibre and the colour choice is

Sinamay picture hat.

FOR THIS HAT YOU WILL NEED:

A dome block
A large upturn brim block
4 yards (3.5m) black sinamay
1.5 yards (1m) white sinamay
Black and white thread
Pins
Iron
Blocking spring or string/large elastic band
Petersham ribbon
Wire and wire-cutters

huge, with different companies supplying lots of different colour ranges. The beauty of this natural fibre is that it can also be dyed easily at home using commercial dyes that can be bought from most hardware shops and departments. This sophisticated and elegant sinamay hat is suitable for a host of different occasions and you can customize it yourself by using your own choice of colours and trimmings. For this hat we will be using the pull-down method.

First of all, take your head measurement (*see* Chapter 4) and then select your blocks. This hat block has a deep upturn which produces a feature on the right-hand side, giving an elegant asymmetrical effect across the brow. The crown block is a standard dome block, which is very versatile and is an excellent starter block.

Blocking the Hat

Start with the brim. Measure across the width of the block both ways and add 1.5in (4cm) on both sides, ensuring that the tape measure is allowed to rest in the dip as opposed to being pulled taut. Using the longest measurement, cut

ESSENTIAL SKILLS:

For this hat it may be useful to refer to Chapter 4 to find out how to take a head measurement, make up a headribbon, sew with wire, slip, tacking and back stitches, find the true bias and use the pull-down method.

Also refer to the blocked sinamay headpiece in Chapter 7 for pinning a sinamay binding.

Asymmetrical brim block.

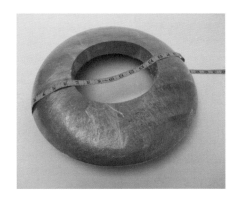

1. Measure across your block.

2. Use the dome block to help create the headfitting.

3. Mark 1in (2.5cm) in from the edge.

4. Cut along the pencil line.

5. Clip at all four straight grain points and pin.

6. Pull the sinamay down over the dome block.

7. Tie string around the block to help reduce fullness.

8. Pin the bottom edge all the way around.

three squares of this measurement.

Decide where the centre back (CB) will be and mark it on the block. Many blocks already have it marked, but if not, you can make the decision according to the shape. Having cut your three squares of sinamay, stretch each one across the bias weave (the diagonal) in both directions, returning it to its original shape afterwards (*see* Chapter 4).

If there is a lot of stiffener in the sinamay it is best to spray it with tap water to soften it as this makes the stretching easier and helps ensure it doesn't rip. Most sinamay comes ready stiffened these days but there are differences in the quality, so if the material feels very soft it will need stiffening. The easiest way is to use water-based stiffener. The alternative is to use straw stiffener, which is like a varnish and can be applied before or after blocking. This method is shown in the parisisal pillbox hat.

If you are using ready-stiffened sinamay, spray each square with water and lay on a flat surface in a diamond or rhombus shape so that the bias is at the top, bottom and sides. Then line up the grains so that they match the one beneath. This ensures it looks neat and professional, and maintains the transparent element of the sinamay which is part of its charm and character. The hat should look and feel light and airy.

It is sometimes helpful to rest the brim block on top of another smaller block, or alternatively a biscuit tin or similar. This gives space to be able to pin under the edge of the block easily. Lay the squares over the block with the bias top corner at the CB point. Smooth the rest over the block so it hangs down over the sides and beyond the line of the edge of the brim.

Using the dome block upside down, gently press the middle of the sinamay square down into the head-shaped hole in the block (the 'headfitting') and take it away.

Next, pin around the outer edge of the block. Start to pin at each of the four areas of the straight grain. Always start with the straight grain when using the pull-down method. Put three or four pins in each of the straight grains, smoothing the opposite sides as you work. When these are secure, pull the centre section of the bias to produce a curve over the block. Then smoothly and evenly pin each segment between the bias point and the side straight grain, then do the same on the other side of the point so the fullness is eased equally and the sinamay lies flat to the block. From time to time press with the heel of your hand into the headfitting area to keep the sinamay slightly dipped. Once you have pinned all around the outer edge, check there are no bumps or lumps. Any slightly raised areas should disappear as the sinamay dries, but making sure the pins are put in firmly and securely, and pulling and smoothing the material as you pin will help to eliminate them.

Next measure 1in (2.5cm) in from the headfitting edge and mark with a coloured marker pencil, thus creating a new inner oval shape.

Cut the oval out along this line with small sharp scissors. Sinamay has a loose weave, making it easy to push the point of sharp scissors in to start the cutting. This oval piece need not be wasted – it can be kept and used as a fascinator base.

At the headfitting, clip at all four straight grain points. Stretch each bias section and pin against the block. This creates the headfitting where the headribbon will be sewn. There is no need to make more clips at this stage.

Once it is completely dry, iron the whole block with a hot iron. Placing a piece of spare sinamay between the iron and the hat acts as a pressing cloth and protects against both the transference of any dirt from the base of the iron and any loose dye from the sinamay. Once you have ironed the block, the CB can be marked with either a tailor's tack in contrasting coloured thread or a large quilter's pin. Leave on the block at this stage.

Next the crown is blocked. Take the longest measurement over the dome block (which is usually front to back as our heads are oval, not round, in circumference). Add 3in (8cm) extra and then cut three squares of this measurement. Stretch the sinamay both ways across the bias and match the grains up as you did with the brim material. The block should have the CB marked. Spray with water to soften. Line the top corner of the diamond shape (the bias point) against the CB, place your hand on the centre of the crown (the tip) and pull down all the way round.

With the straight grains lying straight (vertical), pin these firmly under the block. Push three or four pins into each area. The sinamay needs to be tight-fitting to the block. Tying string around the block or rolling down a large elastic band will help to flatten it.

Now pull the bias corners and pin from the centre of each bias point towards the straight grain as smoothly and evenly as possible and then do the same the other way, going round until it is all pinned. There will be creases, and the area where the straight grain joins a bias may well not lie flat. When it is dry, iron the whole dome block using an extra piece of sinamay as a pressing cloth as you did with the brim, and press the bumpy areas flat. Do not remove from the block at this stage.

You can now return to the brim block and remove the pins.

Making the Headfitting

Remove all the pins from the brim block and lift the sinamay away from the block. If the sinamay layers begin to separate a little at this stage, put a large quilter's pin in to hold them together. Next you need to make sure the CB is marked; this is important so you know which way the hat faces when it is worn, and it is essential for knowing where to place the back seam of your petersham ribbon. Next make up a headribbon (*see* Chapter 4).

Once you have made the headribbon, match the seam up with the CB mark that you made on the headfitting and pin it in place with long, fine pins such as dressmaker's pins. Make sure that the seam allowances (the wings) face the sinamay. Pin downwards along the grain of the petersham. Rest the sinamay brim on your arm as you do this, holding the ribbon at the headfitting so you can work round with the hat supported. Pin all the way round so the edge of the ribbon sits next to the crease made by

blocking the headfitting.

Using a single thread, sew in place with a tiny back stitch, with each stitch two or three grooves along from the previous one. The idea is not to be able to see these stitches on the finished hat, so this is what you're aiming for. It is quite a slow process but it is best to make it as firm as you can. If your first attempt is visible, don't worry as long as it is secure. For a more thorough explanation, *see* Chapter 4.

1. Make the headribbon into a loop.

2. Pin in the headribbon.

3. Sew along the edge of the petersham.

Wire the Brim

To wire the brim, take the measurement around the outer edge of the block (not the blocked sinamay as this may have enlarged a little with handling), starting at the CB mark so you know where you started. For a large hat like this you need a substantial overlap, so add 8in (20cm) to your measurement. Cotton-covered wire comes in either black or white, so choose black for dark colours and cut the wire with wire-cutters. Millinery wire comes packed in a tightly coiled roll, so be careful when you open it that it doesn't spring out dangerously. Once the required length has been cut, reduce the springiness by running your thumb and forefinger along the wire firmly and smoothly, being careful not to apply pressure in short bursts as this will cause

kinks that are really hard to remove. Pushing the wire like this also helps create a circle, particularly if you run the wire over your thumb. Overlap the wire to approximately the brim measurement, checking with the tape measure that it is

correct, and tape the middle with Sellotape.

Lay the wire in the crease created by the blocking to see how well it fits; once you're satisfied, cut away the excess sinamay. Put the wire to one side while

1. Place the wire at the edge of the sinamay brim.

2. Sew in the wire.

you carefully cut along the crease line. Now place the wire along the inside of the sinamay right next to the edge, lining up the centre of the overlap with the CB point.

Sew with wire stitch (see Chapter 4). Start beyond the overlap and sew along the wire until you reach the other end of the overlap. At this point, check that the wire fits comfortably. If necessary you can adjust the length by pulling the free ends of the wire to make it smaller or pushing them to make it bigger. When you're satisfied, tape the wire together so that it can't work loose. Next you can sew the rest of the wire in place. The taped section must be firmly sewn so the wire doesn't work its way out and stick through the binding.

Binding

The next step is to create the binding. Take the remaining sinamay and, if you haven't already stretched it both ways on the bias, do so now, making sure that you pull it back to its original shape to ensure it doesn't become too narrow when you've ironed it into a binding. To find the true bias across the whole width of the material, fold the selvedge across at 45 degrees and line it up against the straight grain, the weft of the weave. This creates the true bias. (Finding the true bias is explained fully in Chapter 4.) Decide on the width of the binding. If you decide it should be 0.75in (2cm) deep, you will need to cut four times that depth to allow for the folding in on both sides. If you decide to include the bias fold you've just made in your measurement (this can be useful as you'll need a centre fold for the binding anyway), then take this into consideration when cutting enough for your desired width. When cutting, make sure it is long enough to go around the brim. Next, fold it in half lengthways, and in again on both sides, so there are

1. Fold the sinamay in on both sides.

2. The finished binding.

no spiky (cut) edges and it is deep enough to cover the wire and look smart.

You can achieve this neat fold using a hot iron, which will activate the stiffener. If it doesn't lay flat straight away, a quick spray of water and then pressing with the iron will perfect the finish.

Lay the sinamay bind evenly on either side of the wired edge, smoothing gently and easing as you follow the curve. Pin at regular intervals with long pins, pushing the pins lengthways so they are at right angles to the edge as this produces far less puckering. (This pinning method is illustrated in the blocked sinamay headpiece in Chapter 7.) Tack with a contrasting thread to secure, and remove the pins (for tacking, see Chapter 4). Fold the end under so that no cut edges can be seen and it gives a neat seam ending. This can be either a straight seam or it can follow the bias. (You can see examples of both in Chapter 7.) Sew with a matching thread in slip stitch to hold the binding in place and press with a hot iron for a perfect finish.

Attaching the Crown to the Brim

To begin, line up the CB mark you made on the crown with the one you made on the brim. Overlap the crown over the

headfitting so it sits in line with the stitching of the petersham. The crown should fit comfortably over the entire headfitting. Pin the crown to the sinamay of the headfitting, holding the petersham out of the way.

Thread the needle with double thread of a matching colour about 20in (50cm) long with a knot at the end. Starting at CB, sew the crown to the brim with a long back stitch, making sure the petersham isn't in the way. Make a stitch about 0.75in (2cm) long, then come back halfway and make another stitch of the same size. This overlapping strengthens the stitching and prevents any movement between crown and brim. Continue sewing around the crown until you have returned to CB. Finish off securely with an extra back stitch.

Pin the crown to the brim.

Trimming

The stitching on the crown needs to be hidden, and this is where the trimming comes in useful. Take a wide piece of sinamay the length of the headfitting and fold in both sides so it looks soft, without any cut edges showing. Make a small pleat at one end; holding this in place on the right-hand side of the crown, bring the rest around the crown so it fits snugly but not too tightly.

Pleat the other end and cut where needed to sew the two pleated ends together. Oversew using double thread. This creates a circle of sinamay that is not actually attached to the hat at this stage and so is still movable. There is no need to overlap the sinamay as this only makes it bulky. The sinamay circle now needs to be covered and more trimming added.

For the trimming, black and white curled sinamay has been used. This covers the cut ends and creates a jaunty

1. Don't sew the trim to the crown at this stage.

2. Black and white sinamay swirls.

3. Sew the quills in place.

4. Add the trim.

design that balances the large upturn on the opposite side of the hat. This is a very useful trimming technique. Take a bias strip of the full width of the sinamay approximately 4in (10cm) wide. Fold it in half and iron before opening up again to turn both sides into the middle and iron again. Lastly iron the two sides together to ensure no raw edges are showing. If at any point the sinamay doesn't stick together, spray it with a little tap water. The strip is then bound around a long cardboard tube and steamed if a little dry. Do this with both the black and the white sinamay strips.

When it is dry, remove the sinamay from the cardboard tube to give a long, corkscrew effect. Cut these two lengths in half so that you have four equal curls that can be arranged decoratively over the join of the headband to form the trimming on the right-hand side of the crown. Cut the ends of the sinamay at an angle along the bias grain to create a sharp point. Next, pin in place and sew to the hat using tie tacks in matching thread.

As a finishing touch, add two ivory quills across the front of the hat, resting from left to right. Glue the two quills together at the point where they will be attached to the hat. When the glue is dry, push a large pin all the way through to create two large holes through the quills. Using double thread, sew through these holes to attach the quills to the hat so that no thread shows on the outside of the quills.

A picture hat is always striking regardless of the materials used and it will always make a big statement. Here are some more examples from different contemporary milliners.

Rizvi Millinery. Veil of Illusion Collection. Style: Tatto. Photographer: Ness Sherry. Model Iona Montgomery.

Judy Bentinck Millinery. Mantalini Collection. Cerise pink parisisal picture hat. Photographer: Alistair Cowin. Model: Daisy.

Judy Bentinck Millinery. Under the Rainbow Collection. Pewter and silver window sinamay picture hat. Photographer: Alistair Cowin. Model: Amy Macdonald.

Keely Hunter Millinery. Shapka Collection. Style: white large brim. Photographer: Peter Fingleton.

Judy Bentinck Millinery. Coco Rococo Collection. Style: large panama sun hat. Photographer: Alistair Cowin. Model: Amy Macdonald.

Cloche Hats

A cloche hat is a tight fitting hat that sits snugly on the head, with a small brim that is turned down over the face. Sometimes the brim is turned up on one side. Cloche is the French word for bell, which is the perfect description for the shape of this hat. It rose to popularity in the 1920s when short hairstyles for women were very fashionable, the Eton crop being a good example. This was the period when the 'Flappers' were at the height of their popularity too. They had a boyish look with short, straight unfitted dresses with a low waistline (the opposite of figure-hugging). Felt was the ideal material for the cloche shape but these hats could also be made in straw or sisal for the summer and with lace and beading for evening wear. Cloche hats went out of fashion towards the end of the 1920s but enjoyed a brief revival in the 1960s. Nowadays a slightly less head-hugging version is a flattering and easy-to-wear style, as shown below.

A wool felt cone is a preformed hood made of sheep's wool that has been processed in a factory to create a fully bonded wool fibre shape and then dyed to produce a large range of different colours.

This cloche hat is made using two

Wool felt cloche.

FOR THIS HAT YOU WILL NEED:

Two wool felt cones (in this instance one pink, one navy)
Two blocks (one cloche brim block, one straight-sided crown)
Black millinery wire
Navy 1in (2.5cm) wide petersham (no. 5)
Navy and pink threads
Needle and pins
Clingfilm

wooden blocks and two felt cones of different colours. The wool felt is very reasonably priced and easy to work with, so is a good material to use, particularly for a beginner.

Blocking the Hat

Start by choosing your blocks. This example uses a cloche brim block and a straight-sided standard crown block. Cover both blocks with cling film as smoothly as possible, as creases will

ESSENTIAL SKILLS:

For this hat it may be useful to refer to Chapter 4 to find out how to make up a headribbon, sew with back, long back, oversew, wire and tacking stitches, and make a petersham binding. Refer to Chapter 9 for felt trims.

1. Place the felt over the cloche brim block.

2. Measure the required depth.

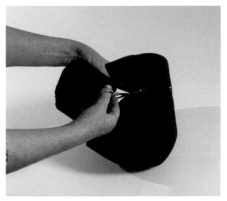

3. Cut along the pin mark.

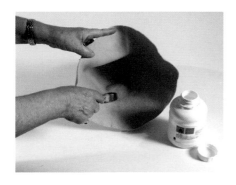

4. Paint with felt stiffener.

5. Pin along the lower edge first.

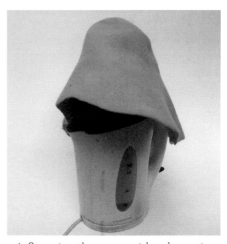

6. Steaming the crown with a domestic kettle.

show through and can spoil the smoothness of the felt when blocked.

Starting with the brim (crowns can be extended but brims cannot), put the felt cone over the block. In this case navy wool felt has been used.

Decide on the depth of your brim; here 4in (10cm) was used. Before you cut the felt for the brim, add 1.5in (4cm) to this measurement as an allowance.

Mark where you're going to cut with a line of pins, or you can tack (baste) along this line if you want to be more accurate. Then cut along the marked line.

Next stiffen the felt with felt stiffener. This is like a varnish and should be applied sparingly but evenly. Using a small household paintbrush, dip it into the stiffener and then wipe it carefully to remove any excess. Always brush inside the hood and never on the outside. Use it sparingly: more stiffener can be added later if more strength is needed. This method will be repeated later with the crown.

Allow the stiffened felt to dry thoroughly. If any moisture touches the stiffener while it is still damp, it will leave white marks that are difficult to

7. Pin the felt to the block.

remove. While the brim felt is drying, start working on the crown; in this case a pink felt cone has been used. Pull the cone over the block to check that it fits comfortably. Take the cone off the block and paint the stiffener onto the inside in a circular motion, working it evenly into the felt. Leave it to dry. No measuring or cutting is done with the crown felt at this stage.

Once the navy brim felt is dry, it can be blocked. First wipe the inside with a damp cloth, or briefly spray with water to dampen it. Next steam the felt; holding it over a household kettle is fine if you don't have a professional steamer. Keep it over the steam until bubbles of moisture appear on the outside of the felt, rather like condensation. Keep the felt moving and turning in the steam, as this distributes the moisture evenly and softens it, but take care not to scald your hands. Using a pair of tongs or a wooden spoon inside can help control this movement. Continue until the felt is really soft and pliable.

Lay the felt over the block and pull it down firmly all around. Pin the lower edge first. Decide where the centre back (CB) is and mark it. This helps you know which way the hat will be worn when it is completed. As you pin in, use your thimble to push the pins in firmly and then pull back to add more purchase at each pin.

It is sometimes easier to pin at the four compass points and then ease and pin the felt between these points. The rest of the felt is then pinned at the top edge, which is the headfitting. Pull and smooth the felt up into this smaller measurement. The top edge (headfitting) can be uneven at this stage, as it will be trimmed down after the crown is attached. A wet cloth can be applied and pressed with a hot iron to help achieve the correct shape. Heat and water are essential to shrink or stretch the felt to produce a perfect flat finish.

When the pinning is complete, check for wrinkles; if they are slight, they are likely to disappear while the felt dries. If you can see any, then take the pins out at that section and pull again to make the felt flatter. Then brush the damp felt with a soft brush around the shape. This gives a professional look as all the fibres lie in the same direction. Leave it to dry. The shape will set and hold even once it is removed from the block.

1. Pin and sew the headribbon.

2. Sew with a tiny backstitch.

3. Sew the taped wire to the felt brim.

4. Tack the binding in place.

5. Wipe with a damp cloth.

Now block the pink crown felt. Dampen the inside with a wet cloth or give a quick spray with water as you did with the brim and follow the same steps to soften it by holding the felt over the steam until bubbles appear on the outside.

When it is ready, place the felt over the crown block and pull it down firmly all around. The bottom edge will flare out but it isn't a problem at this stage. Clearly mark the CB. If the tip (top) has wrinkles and won't lie flat to the block, place a wet cloth over it and press with a hot iron. Then remove both and pull down hard, smoothing the tip over at the same time. To help with this process, a large elastic band can be rolled down or a double string can be used. Alternatively you can use a blocking spring. This helps reduce the excess felt, making it easier to then pin the felt.

Pin evenly along the bottom edge; household pins are ideal as they can be put close together but alternative and easier ways are to use drawing pins or red blocking pins (these can be purchased from millinery suppliers). Leave to dry thoroughly.

Any excess felt will be cut off after the depth of the crown has been decided. Make sure you keep the remaining felt as this can be used for trimming or for creating a felt fascinator.

Working with the Brim

When the brim is completely dry, unpin and remove the felt from the block. This should be easy to do in one movement. If it is difficult to remove, run a kitchen palette knife around the inside; this will release it and it should pop off easily. Making sure you still have the CB mark, make up your headribbon to the measurement suitable for the wearer (see Chapter 4). Pin the petersham ribbon in place so the edge rests next to the crease line on the felt. Pin lengthways. Using matching thread, sew with a tiny backstitch, as outlined in Chapter 4.

The wire goes in next. From the CB, measure around the bottom edge and add 4in (10cm) as an overlap. Cut the wire to this length with wire-cutters and run your finger and thumb along the length of the cut wire to reduce the springiness. Next run your thumb along the underside of the wire to help curve it into the shape you need. Overlap to the desired amount and then, using

Sellotape, tape the wire into a circle but leave the cut ends of the wire free so that you can adjust the size later if needed. Lay the wire into the crease in the felt to check that the measurement is right; adjustments can be made later. The hat is going to be bound with petersham so the excess felt on the bottom edge needs to be cut away. Cut along the crease line which was made from the blocking. Next, the wire is sewn to this cut edge. Place the wire so the overlap is central to the CB mark.

Starting to one side of the taped overlap, sew with a single thread in wire stitch (*see* Chapter 4). Sew all around the hat until you reach the other end of the overlap again and check it is the correct measurement and that the wire is sitting comfortably. When you're satisfied, tape both free cut ends of the wire so they are controlled and smooth. Sew over the overlap and finish off your stitching.

Make up the matching petersham into a loop as in Chapter 4 and then, matching up the CBs, pin into place around the edge. The petersham should

be equal on both sides of the edge to create a good finish. Stab the pins through, then tack (baste) with a contrasting thread close to the edge with a stitch about 0.5in (1cm) long all the way around.

The petersham will look bumpy at this stage. Remove the pins as you tack. The tacking is merely a holding stitch and will be removed. Dampen a soft cloth and wipe evenly around the ribbon. This removes all the bumps as the petersham shrinks to fit. Sew this on with a matching single thread using stab stitch.

Attaching the Crown to the Brim

Decide on the depth of the crown and mark it with pins; in this example it is 4in (10cm). Remove the felt from the block and cut along this pinned line.

Matching the CB marks, place the crown over the brim headfitting and pin all the way around, holding the headribbon out of the way. Make sure the crown is straight. Sew together with double thread and a long backstitch.

1. Mark the height and remove the felt from the block.

2. Pin the crown to the brim.

Trimming the Hat

The detail created for this hat is a simple bow of 1in (2.5cm) wide pink felt intertwined with three loops of navy felt to create a good colour balance.

Start by taking the leftover piece of pink felt from blocking the crown and cut a strip 1in (2.5cm) wide to the headfitting measurement. It should rest comfortably around the crown. Sew the ends edge to edge with a big oversew stitch and double thread. This detail will cover up the crown and brim join. It is best not to overlap because this will just add unwanted bulk. Next, cut another strip 1in (2.5cm) wide and long enough to create a generous bow. Make this strip into a bow with one end cut to a point.

Similarly, take the leftover piece of navy felt that was cut off after blocking the brim, and using a wet cloth and a hot iron flatten the remaining felt out in sections by laying the wet cloth onto the felt and pressing with the iron on its hottest setting for ten seconds. Remove and then pull the felt both ways, which will straighten it out and remove the wavy shapes. Finally cut a strip 1in (2.5cm) wide, long enough to create the loops.

Next, intertwine the navy strip through the pink bow, sewing through to the pink felt covering the join of the crown. Taking a 3in (8cm) strip of the pink felt, wind this around the middle section of the bow and join. Slide this join to the back so that it cannot be seen and sew this to the hat from the inside of the crown. This trimming has been placed over the right eye, lending interest to the front and the side of the hat.

This style hat can also be made up with a number of different straws or fabrics. Both crown and brim can be modified but the essential cloche style will always remain.

Smoothing out the felt.

The finished hat.

Judy Bentinck Millinery. Lorelei Collection. Style: turquoise parisisal cloche with velvet trim. Photographer: Alistair Cowin. Model: Emily Healey.

Atelier Millinery. Style: blue wool felt cloche with petersham trim.

Judy Bentinck Millinery. Portia Collection. Style: printed aubergine wool felt cloche. Photographer: Alistair Cowin. Model: Lucy Shropshall.

Judy Bentinck Millinery. Style: brown wool felt cloche with shot silk bow. Photographer: Alistair Cowin. Model: Tamlyn Williams.

Lyze Hats. Style: Jaeda.

Knotted Sisal and Pinok Pok Bowler Hat

The Bowler Hat

The bowler is a quintessentially English style statement and, although its wide use as a businessman's hat has died out since the 1970s, the image remains iconic. Bowler-shaped hats are now worn by both men and women, with the original hard hat bowler still worn by many sporting officials.

Originally the bowler was designed to be worn by gamekeepers. The story goes that a close relation of the Earl of Leicester decided that the gamekeepers at their Holkham Hall Estate in Norfolk needed hard hats to protect their heads from low-hanging branches. William Coke asked Lock's hatters of St James in London to create a hat to fit this brief. They went to Thomas Bowler in south London, who did in fact produce the perfect hat. Coke apparently tested its suitability by stamping on it; as it didn't collapse, the design was deemed a success.

Initially the hat was called the 'Coke', but once the style had been established by Bowler it took the manufacturer's name. In America the bowler is known as the 'Derby', and they are often brown.

Pinok pok bowler hat.

FOR THIS HAT YOU WILL NEED:

One knotted sisal capeline/hood
1 yard (1m) pinok pok
A bowler block
A flat buckram block as an alternative to wood
Petersham ribbon in two colours
Millinery wire
Thread
A kitchen palette knife or corset bone
Cling film (saran wrap)

Blocking the Brim

For the brim of this bowler hat we are using a high-quality straw called pinok pok. It has a tight weave that makes it very good quality, but can also make it slightly more difficult to work with. It does not have the same 'give' as sinamay, although it is woven in the same way. The block used here has been created with layers of buckram that have

ESSENTIAL SKILLS:

For this hat it may be useful to refer to Chapter 4 to find out how to make up a headribbon, sew with back, long back, wire, stab, long running and oversew stitches, and make a petersham binding.

been wired and roped together, producing a substantially strong block, though less durable than a wooden one.

Measure across the block to find the widest point and then add 2in (5cm). In this case two squares 16in (41cm) across have been cut. This needs to be stiffened with water-based stiffener. This is a substance a little like PVA craft glue but not as sticky. Before you start to stiffen, lay out a few sheets of kitchen towel or paper hand towels. For the brim, dilute the stiffener in the proportion of 1 part to 4 parts water. You can use the cap as a measure. In this case two measures of stiffener is enough. Pour this into a clean plastic bowl. Now measure eight capfuls of water and mix thoroughly with a spoon, making sure there are no lumps of stiffener left. It must be well mixed in, as any unmixed stiffener is very difficult to remove once the hat has been blocked. Submerge the squares of pinok pok in the stiffener and then remove and roll up.

Leave the rolls on the clean paper towels for a minute or two. Unroll and blot to remove any surface stiffener.

Having marked the centre back (CB) on the block, lay the block on top of the square of pinok pok with the bias point at CB. Pin there and opposite at centre front (CF) to hold, and then pin opposing sides at the straight grains. Next finish pinning at the bias points and all the way round, pulling firmly to lose all the fullness. Leave to dry.

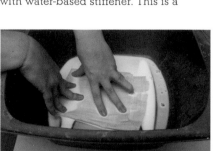

1. Submerge the pinok pok squares in the stiffener and then roll them up and leave to become tacky.

2. Blot with paper towels.

3. Pin at the bias point to hold in place and then on all opposing straight grains.

4. Pin the brim block all the way round.

5. Pin the brim block all the way round.

Blocking the Crown

For the crown, a natural knotted sisal hood has been used. This also needs to be stiffened, so make up your solution in the same way as for the brim. Before you start, lay out a few sheets of fresh kitchen towel or paper hand towels. With the straw hood folded in half lengthways, carefully submerge it in the liquid. Move the hood around and turn it so it has equal contact with the stiffener all over. Remove from the bowl and lay it on the paper towels. Leave for a minute or two to soak in. Then blot with a piece of paper towel to ensure no stiffener is left on the surface. Do this all over the hood.

Make sure the bowler block has fresh cling film on it. Pull the hood over the block, keeping the centre of the hood on the centre of the tip of the block (that's the very middle bit) – there is a woven detail that makes lining this up easy. Push firmly down the block, smoothing and pulling as you go. Pin at CB, CF and sides, and then roll the blocking spring down to help hold the straw in place.

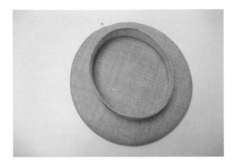

1. Mark the correct-sized headfitting.

2. Mark both ovals with a contrasting thread.

3. Pin in the headribbon.

4. Lay the wire in the folded edge.

5. The wire sewn in place.

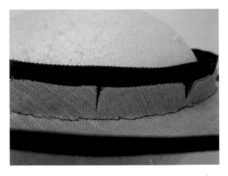

6. Clip the pinok pok at regular intervals around the headfitting.

Block the sisal firmly and evenly.

Pull the straw below the spring to make it really smooth to the block with no wrinkles showing. Pin all the way around and leave to dry. The textured pattern in the weave should look straight and even. There will be quite a lot of excess sisal, but this will be cut off later. Leave the crown on the block for now, so that it doesn't lose its shape.

Completing the Brim

Return to the brim once it is dry. While it is still on the block, mark the headfitting according to your required size, ensuring that it matches the crown. Mark this oval with a fabric marker and then measure in 1.25in (3cm) from that line and mark another, smaller oval. Remove the pins from the block and

carefully lift the brim off, keeping the CB marked. Tack along both these oval lines with a contrasting coloured thread so it can be seen clearly on both sides.

Cut along the smaller line. If you cut out the middle in one piece, this can be used for a fascinator base at another time.

Using small, sharp scissors, cut on each of the four straight grains towards the marked line for the headfitting, being careful not to cut across the line. These cuts are known as 'clips'. You will need to do more clipping at a later stage with this hat.

Make up the headribbon to the correct size (see Chapter 4) and, starting at CB, pin the ribbon in place.

Sew with a tiny backstitch at the edge of the ribbon along the tack line. Then measure the outer edge of the brim, add 5in (13cm) and then cut the wire to that length.

Cut away the excess pinok pok about 0.25in (1cm) in from the blocked edge and then lay the wire inside this folded edge. Sew in using wire stitch over the top of the wire and pinok pok using a matching thread.

Next measure the outside of the wired edge of the brim and add 2in (5cm) to this measurement. Cut this length in millinery petersham. Join the two ends to make a CB seam, using the small oversew stitch to create a loop (see Chapter 4). Fit this petersham loop over the wired edge and pin in place. Then tack in place and take the pins out. Run a damp cloth along both sides of the petersham and leave to dry. It will shrink to fit and shouldn't have any creases. Now sew the petersham on with stab stitch.

Clip at regular intervals (about every 2in/5cm) all around the headfitting. The pinok pok has very little give but these clips will ensure the headribbon fits comfortably to the head.

The brim is now ready to be attached to the crown.

Attaching the Crown to the Brim

Once the crown is dry, you need to decide on its finished height. In this case, 1in (2.5cm) has been measured above the bottom of the block. Pin to mark this line. Next, using a kitchen palette knife or a plastic corset bone, run the blade under the stiffened crown to release it from the block. The corset bone can slide up and over the tip of the crown so is very useful. Make sure the CB is marked before the crown comes off the block. Away from the block, cut the crown to the height that you've marked.

Pin the crown to the brim all around, matching the CB marks, holding the headribbon out of the way. Once it is pinned, sew with double thread using a long backstitch as shown in Chapter 4.

Steam the brim gently with the kettle and then, using both hands equally, curve the sides of the brim up at both sides to produce as close to the classic bowler shape as you can. Check the curves are equal from all angles.

Sew the crown to the brim.

Trimming the Hat

Strips of 1in (2.5cm) wide brown and beige petersham have been used here to create the hatband that covers the crown and the brim join. Cut the length so that it fits comfortably around the outside of the crown. The beige has been sandwiched between two lengths of the brown petersham, creating a narrow stripe. These three pieces of petersham are joined together with a long running

Iron the petersham binding to curve it.

stitch of matching brown thread at the back and a tiny stitch at the front. Press the top edge with a steam iron to shape and shrink it slightly so that it fits snugly around the crown.

Join the two ends, ensuring it isn't attached to the hat at this stage. Make sure that the stripe is level and the same width all the way round.

Next, create the detail by cutting a yard or metre of each coloured petersham ribbon and looping to create a loose rosette shape.

First, decide where the detail should sit and then, centring the detail over the joined petersham, sew all the way through the hat to hold everything in place. Fish-tail the ends for a perfect finish.

This timeless bowler style looks good with any number of trims, both bold and subtle. Overleaf there are some more examples to inspire you.

Making a looped rosette trim.

The finished hat.

Judy Bentinck Millinery. Coco Rococo Collection. Style: white sinamay bowler with satin-covered brim. Photographer: Alistair Cowin. Model: Amy Macdonald.

Rizvi Millinery. Wild at Heart Collection. Style: heart bowler. Photographer: Suelan. Model: Natascha.

Judy Bentinck Millinery. Style: Jubilee bowler decorated with red, white and blue satin trim.

Judy Bentinck Millinery. Under the Rainbow Collection. Style: pastel green sinamay bowler.
Photographer: Alistair Cowin. Model: Amy Macdonald.

Silk Dupion-covered Cocktail Hat

Cocktail Hats

These are small decorative hats that don't necessarily cover the whole head. It is the nearest a hat can be to a fascinator or headpiece, the difference being that it has a headribbon, so it is classed as a hat even if it doesn't fit over the whole crown. Originally these hats were worn to cocktail parties, hence the name. Nowadays they are worn to weddings, race days and other special events, but the name has remained the same. They are often elaborately decorated and may have a full veil across the face or just over the eyes. They were particularly popular in the 1940s and early 1950s, when everyone wore a hat wherever they went. These little hats are easy to wear and have become popular with the younger members of the royal family. As they have no brim, the face is not shaded or obscured in any way, so they are perfect for photographers at weddings or for the Press.

Silk dupion-covered cocktail hat.

FOR THIS HAT YOU WILL NEED:

A button block (this example used a 7.5in tip, mini block)
Clingfilm
0.5 yards (0.5m) canvas
Interfacing
1 yard (1m) navy silk dupion
0.5 yards (0.5m) ivory silk dupion
Narrow petersham
A large button
Thread

Fabric Hats

More steps are involved in the making of a fabric hat than in one of felt or straw as a fabric hat needs a foundation fabric, an interfacing and the chosen outer fabric. They also need to be lined to cover up the foundation, which gives a beautiful finish to an already detailed hat.

Blocking the Hat

First choose your block. In this example, a button block has been used. Measure across the little block and cut a generous square of single canvas (the measurement plus 2in/5cm).

Wipe the canvas evenly with a damp

ESSENTIAL SKILLS:

For this hat it may be useful to refer to Chapter 4 to find out how to make and sew a headribbon, join fabric bias strips and sew with stab, back, running and gathering stitches.

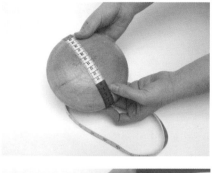

1. Cut a rectangle of silk.

2. Join the vertical seam at centre back.

Measure the block.

Iron the stayflex interfacing to the canvas.

3. Ease the fabric over the block.

cloth (not too wet – you don't want to soak it), and leave it to become soft and a bit tacky. Cover the block with fresh clingfilm. Block the canvas over and pin the straight grains first, working the bias areas next, pushing out as many creases

as possible.

Use the back of a knife blade to push out any wrinkles. This a very effective method. Once you've done this, leave the canvas to dry. Meanwhile make up your headribbon with narrow petersham to the appropriate size (*see* Chapter 4). The headribbon used on this hat is the size of the inner part of the block.

Next measure out a piece of stayflex interfacing the same size as the canvas. The interfacing is ironed onto the dry canvas while it is still on the block, and its purpose is to stop the texture of the canvas showing through your silk fabric. Take a hot iron and iron until the material is smooth, pulling carefully to remove as many creases as possible, particularly on the underside of the block.

Pin the canvas carefully over the block.

Working with Fabric

Take the measurement of the outer edge of the block and cut a bias rectangle of

4. Pin the fabric to the block.

the silk. It should measure the depth of the block from the pinning line beneath the block to the centre of the tip, plus 1in (2.5cm). In this example the fabric measures 20 × 5.5in (51 × 14cm).

Iron this rectangle to remove any creases and then make it into a loop and

5. Gather along the top and stitch.

6. Sew a tack line to hold the layers together.

sew a centre back (CB) seam (see the image of the vertical seam in Joining Bias Strips in Chapter 4).

Iron the CB seam open. Ease this loop of fabric over the block to cover the interfacing, with the CB seam on the silk fabric lined up vertically with the CB mark on the block.

The seam should be flat and open on the inside. Pin into the block on the underside.

Now run a gathering stitch along the top edge of the silk as close to the block as you can, pulling the material towards the centre of the block. Gather the thread up firmly and secure by stitching through the gathers.

Remove the pins at the bottom edge and pull down to 'block' the fabric and make it curve closely to the block. Pull the gathers down smoothly and neatly. It will all be covered up by the detail but it is best to make it lie as flat as possible. Pin and then sew a tack line to hold all the layers together on the underside.

Now remove from the block and cut the excess canvas away to make it easier to handle when putting your headribbon in. Pin your headribbon along the tacking line, ensuring that it won't be seen when worn. Sew with matching thread and tiny stab stitches, as explained in Chapter 4.

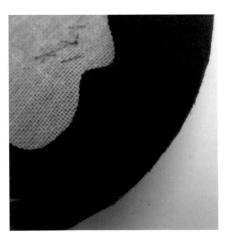

7. Sew in the headribbon.

Making the Trimming

Cut five rectangles of matching dupion 5 × 4in (13 × 10cm). Fold lengthways and machine sew along the long side before turning so that the seam is on the inside of the tube.

Next fold the tube in half so that it is approximately 2.5in (6.5cm) long and fold both ends together with a single pleat. Do this with all five pieces, then arrange the shapes to fan out from the centre of the hat and sew them in place at the centre point of the hat.

Cover a button with ivory silk dupion. (You can buy metal buttons that clip together once the fabric has been positioned.) Sew the button in the centre to cover the ends and create an attractive flower shape on top of the hat.

1. Create the fabric tubes.

2. Create the five pieces for the trimming.

Making the Lining

For this type of hat, the lining always comes last so that you can hide all the stitching. Measure and cut a rectangle of fabric (in this case silk dupion) the same size as the rectangle you made for the outer covering but without the additional seam allowance (so for this example a piece of fabric measuring 19 × 4.5in/48 × 11cm was used). Fold over the top edge by half an inch (1cm); this will be your wrong side. Make the rectangle into a loop by joining with a CB seam which can either be machined or hand sewn with a tiny back stitch. Run a gathering stitch along the folded area, keeping a knot at one end. Do not finish off for now.

Gather up the fabric by pulling gently on the thread, making the hole in the middle as small as possible. Next finish off with the needle and thread. Take this lining fabric with the CB seam showing on the outside and block onto the original button block. To do this, gently steam the fabric, holding the steamer or kettle a good distance away as any droplets of water can stain the silk. This need only be done for a minute or two. Then pull and pin over the block, keeping the gathered centre lined up with the centre of the block. Leave it to dry on the block.

Next you need to make a small covering for the gap in the centre of your lining. Take a small piece of matching silk, draw a 1in (2.5cm) circle using a compass (or draw around a two pence piece) and cut the shape out. Sew in place catching through the gathers with a running stitch.

Once you have done this, check that the lining has fully dried and then unpin and carefully line the CB seam up with the CB of the headribbon on the hat so that the wrong side of the lining sits inside, next to the canvas foundation.

Carefully ease the lining inside and smooth all the way around, lifting the headribbon out of the way to be able to do this. Pin in place and sew with a single thread and a running stitch. Finally trim the excess lining fabric away, then push the headribbon back inside.

Finally sew in a hat elastic under the headribbon so that the hat can be worn at any angle, with the elastic tucked under the wearer's hair.

Cocktail hats lend themselves well to being decorated with interesting fabrics and to having generous trimmings, thereby producing stunning pieces without an imposing big brim. Here are some great examples:

We have covered a good selection of blocked hats in this chapter with ideas to encourage you to create more in your own style. In the next chapter you will be introduced to some stimulating ideas for creating headpieces and fascinators.

1. Block the silk lining.

2. The lining as it will fit into the hat.

3. Lift the headribbon out of the way.

The finished cocktail hat.

Judy Bentinck Millinery. Coco Rococo Collection. Style: black silk dupion cocktail hat with gold hackle/coque/guinea fowl feathers. Photography: Alistair Cowin. Model: Amy Macdonald.

Judy Bentinck Millinery. Scheherezade Collection. Style: blue and pink striped fabric cocktail hat.

Judy Bentinck Millinery. Scheherezade Collection. Style: red and beige striped cocktail hat with large bow.

Rizvi Millinery. Collection: Veil of Illusion. Style: Becky. Photographer: Ness Sherry. Model: Bandury Cross.

Chapter 7
Headpieces and Fascinators

Headpieces and fascinators come in all shapes and sizes, but the thing that sets them apart from hats is the way they're attached to the head. Headpieces and fascinators are made with an alice band, comb or hair clip, while hats have a headfitting and headribbon. Headpieces and fascinators are very popular because they are essentially a little bit of nonsense that can make the wearer feel dressed up and a bit glamorous, without the need for an actual hat. There has been some confusion recently about the difference between a fascinator and a headpiece. In millinery terms they mean the same thing, but if there is a difference at all, the word fascinator tends to refer to smaller pieces that are set on combs or clips. They are usually lightweight and feature feathers, flowers, beads and veiling. The term was first used in the US in the 1860s and referred to a small knitted or crocheted shawl-like scarf worn over the head; some were made of lace. In the past fascinators were also called whimsies or confectioneries. The modern usage of the word was popularised in the UK in 2003 when the Press picked up on the fabulous Philip Treacy fascinator that Victoria Beckham wore to Buckingham Palace when her husband David received his OBE.

This chapter will show seven different ways of creating headpieces, the smaller examples of which have been named fascinators.

Turquoise sinamay fascinator.

Freeform sinamay fascinator.

Red spot fascinator.

Felt fascinator.

Crin headpiece.

Bridal fascinator.

LEFT: Judy Bentinck Millinery. Style: pink blocked sinamay headpiece. Photographer: Alistair Cowin. Model: Tamlyn Williams. Make-up and hair: Sammy Carpenter.

Turquoise Sinamay Fascinator

This piece is very simple to create and therefore is an ideal starting point for a beginner. Begin by making the fascinator base. To do this, cut 21in (53cm) of cotton-covered millinery wire and curve it into your preferred shape; in this case, an oval has been made with a 3.5in (9cm) overlap that will go at the centre back (CB). Using Sellotape, tape the wire at the middle point to hold it together and when you're satisfied with the shape, tape both cut ends to make sure they don't stick out.

Next, take a piece of sinamay 10in (26cm) square and fold along the diagonal bias before cutting along this fold to create two triangular pieces. Spray with water and then iron so that the two pieces stick together. The grains should match. Lay your oval wire shape on top of the sinamay, with the overlap next to the longest straight side. This ensures that you have your bias running the length of the base. Because the bias is the stretchiest part of the material, with the most give, this will assist when you come to shape it over the head.

**FOR THIS FASCINATOR
YOU WILL NEED:**

Ready-stiffened sinamay

1 yard (1m) sinamay

Approx ten coque feathers

Approx eight matching guinea-fowl feathers

White cotton-covered millinery wire

Sellotape

UHU glue

Water spray bottle

Dry iron

Scissors, needle, matching thread and pins (including quilter's)

Clear 4in (10cm) plastic-toothed comb

Alternative to the comb: headband or millinery elastic

Turquoise sinamay fascinator.

Pin the wire to the sinamay using long quilter's pins to hold it in place, then cut around the shape, approximately 0.5in (1cm) outside the wire.

Carefully push the excess sinamay over the wire using your thumbs. If it feels a little bulky, spray with a small amount of water to make it softer and easier to work with. Pin as you go. Make sure the excess turning is fairly equal all the way around. Sew using a matching thread and a quick wire stitch (*see*

Chapter 4), and finish off with a secure stitch. Taking small, sharp scissors, trim

ESSENTIAL SKILLS:

For this hat it may be useful to refer to Chapter 9 to find out how to make a sinamay binding and an ironed sinamay detail, and to Chapter 4 for the quick wire stitch.

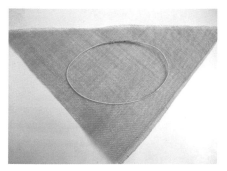

1. Place the made-up wire on your sinamay.

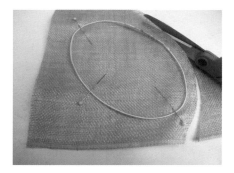

2. Pin in place and cut around the shape.

3. Trim off the excess sinamay.

4. Bind with sinamay.

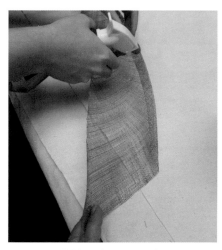

5. Fold and iron the edges.

6. Cut away the excess sinamay.

7. Glue the guinea-fowl feathers to make a flower shape.

8. Coque feathers.

9. Attach the feathers under the sinamay trim.

the excess sinamay down to approximately quarter of an inch (0.5cm), making sure you don't cut into your stitching, and then iron around the outside edge to smooth and flatten the sinamay over the wire. Bind with the same colour sinamay, using the method shown in Chapter 9.

The curve to fit on the side of the head can be shaped over the back of your hand by holding one end with your thumb and curving it over the knuckles to bend it into shape. You can place it on the side of the wearer's head to check the fit and adjust if necessary.

To decorate this particular fascinator, cut a bias strip of matching sinamay 24in (62cm) long by 7in (18cm) wide

and, using a hot iron, fold and iron both sides as shown in the instructions for the Ironed Sinamay Detail in Chapter 9. Turn this into a double loop and stitch together, trimming off any triangular points.

Taking the eight matching guinea-fowl feathers, glue them on to a small circle of sinamay, fanning them out to create a flower-like shape.

Sew the sinamay trim into the middle of the base, attaching the guinea-fowl flower on top to cover all your stitching.

Next, make up two bunches of stripped pale blue coque feathers. The bunches shown have five feathers each. Glue the cut ends together and wrap with a single thread to hold in place. Fan

out to your desired finish.

Carefully push these feathers under the sinamay trim and stitch in place. To finish, add a few guinea-fowl feathers on either side of the coque feathers.

Lastly, attach a clear 4in (10cm) plastic-toothed comb to the inside of the base using double thread in a matching colour. The fascinator is kept in place by pushing the comb into the hair until it feels secure. Alternatively you could sew the base to a headband or use millinery elastic to hold this piece in place.

Here are some other examples of sinamay fascinators to give you further ideas:

Judy Bentinck Millinery. Corona Collection. Style: steel sinamay headpiece with hackle feather spray.

Lyze Hats. Style: Renee. Sinamay fascinator with cut coque feathers and beads.

Judy Bentinck Millinery. Mantalini Collection. Style: black and white rolled sinamay headpiece. Photographer: Alistair Cowin. Model: Daisy.

Blocked Sinamay Headpiece

This beautiful headpiece is easy to wear, as it sits on a wide sinamay-covered headband and adds effortless glamour to an outfit. It can be decorated in a variety of ways to produce very different looks.

Blocking the Hat

Using a purpose-built two piece 'fascinator' block, measure across the block that has the hole in the middle, pressing the tape measure into the dip a little and then adding 1in (2.5cm) on either side. This allows for the stretch when the upper part of the block is pushed into the dip. Taking your sinamay, cut three squares of this measurement. Stretch each piece both ways, then return it to a square shape; there will be a slight curve to the material. Cover both blocks with cling film and then spray the ready-stiffened sinamay with water and leave for a few minutes.

Decide where the centre back (CB) will be and mark it on the lower block (the one with the hole in it). Take the three squares of sinamay, holding them so that the bias is at the top and they make a diamond shape. Lay them over the block with the bias point at the CB and then place the round block in

Blocked sinamay headpiece.

FOR THIS HEADPIECE YOU WILL NEED:

3 yards (3m) sinamay

1 yard (1m) silk dupion (this will make eight flowers)

2 matching quills

Iron

2 piece fascinator block

Scissors, thread, needle, pins

Wide headband

Clingfilm

position over the sinamay. This is what will create the characteristic dipped shape.

Pin at each of the four straight grains first and then, smoothing the material as you go, ease it and pin between these areas. What is useful about this particular block is that it has a string groove that enables you to block more easily by tying a piece of string around the sinamay; the string rests in the groove, thus making the blocking process easier. Make sure the grains are

straight and that all fullness is evenly distributed. When you've pinned all the way around, leave to dry.

ESSENTIAL SKILLS:

For this hat it would be useful to refer to Chapter 4 to find out how to join the wire and sew with the quick wire, slip, tie tack and running stitches, and to Chapter 9 for the sinamay swirls and the silk boat flowers.

1. A two-piece fascinator block.

2. Stretch your sinamay both ways.

3. Place the round block over the sinamay.

4. Tie string around the string groove and pin.

Once the sinamay is dry, lift the top block away and unpin the bottom block. Mark the CB in the sinamay and remove from the block. Measure around the sinamay from the CB pin and add 4in (10cm) to this length. Cut the wire to this measurement. Run the wire through your finger and thumb and curve into a circle, taping at the centre of the overlap. Rest the wire in the crease made by the blocking and press the sinamay over so the wire is inside. Tape both raw ends (*see* Chapter 4 – Joining the Wire) and sew with a quick wire stitch over the top of the sinamay. Trim off the excess sinamay, leaving approximately 0.5in (1cm).

Creating the Self-binding

For your binding, you need to cut a bias strip of sinamay the length of the wired edge plus an overlap (4in/10cm in this case). Then decide how wide you want your finished width to be and multiply this by four as you will be folding it to create the binding. In this case, the strip was 42in (107cm) long by 3in (8cm) (4 × 2cm). Fold your strip in half

Pin the binding in place.

lengthways and iron. Then turn both raw edges into the middle and iron again. It is easier to do this one side at a time. Finally fold together and iron again so that your piece has four layers.

Open it out with your thumbs and, starting at the CB, fit it against the wire so that it sits equally on either side. Spray with a little water to soften it and then curve around the wired shape and pin at regular intervals. Press the sinamay flat to the headpiece, making sure it stays smooth.

To finish at CB you can create a bias seam. To do this, simply fold back along the bias grain, making sure there are no raw edges showing. Cut the excess off, then sew the whole binding with slip stitch at the edge to hold it in place. Next, fold in the ends to make a tiny seam and stitch using slip stitch with matching thread.

Covering the Headband

Next, cover the headband with sinamay. Cut two bias strips of matching sinamay measuring 39 × 1.5in each (1 × 5cm), stretch them both ways and then fold

each in half so that one side is raw, the other side is on the fold. Take one strip and, starting at one end, wrap this around the headband, continuing over the raw edge as you go until you're approximately half way. Pin through to the band securely. Starting again at the other end, wrap in the same way all the way along to join up. If there are raw edges or it doesn't quite fit, you can always cover the join with a folded piece of sinamay without any raw edges. Sew in place neatly using a double thread and running stitch.

Making and Attaching the Trimmings

The next step is to make your trimmings and attach them to the headpiece. This step always takes place before attaching the blocked headpiece to the headband because determining the angle of the headpiece is crucial to the overall look. See Chapter 9 for information on the sinamay swirls and silk boat flowers.

Once you have created (or bought) your trimmings, you need to attach them to the headpiece. For this hat we have

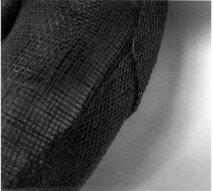

Make a seam on the bias.

Cover the headband with sinamay.

made silk dupion flowers. When attaching them to the blocked base, the back of the flower and the stitching will show through the sinamay. To improve the look, sew the flowers with matching double thread onto a separate small semi-circle of double-layered sinamay which just covers the stitching of the flowers.

Make a base for your flowers from a small semi-circle of sinamay.

When this shape is sewn onto the blocked base, it will hide the back of the flowers. If the sinamay grains are matched up perfectly, it will hardly be noticeable. This method is an easy way to attach a group of flowers to a hat. Again, using matching double thread, pin and sew the semi-circle in the desired position on the upper curve of the base, sewing all the way through the headpiece with a secure stitch.

Sew the flower to the fascinator.

To finish, repeat this method with the remaining flowers, sewing them on the other side of the fascinator disc.

Attaching the Headband to the Headpiece

Now the headband needs to be sewn to the headpiece in three places to prevent it wobbling. It is important at this stage to make sure that the headpiece is sitting at the correct angle. When positioning the headpiece ready to attach to the headband, it is best to ensure that it doesn't touch the wearer's shoulder or obscure the face. Once you are satisfied, pin where the headpiece is to be sewn.

Sew firmly with double thread but as unobtrusively as possible on both sides

Pin where the headpiece is to be sewn onto the headband.

and through all the layers in the middle. The headpiece needs to be secure so it doesn't move about.

Finishing Touches

Lastly, the piece is finished with the matching sinamay swirl and quills. The sinamay swirl can cover any stitching that shows after attaching the headband. The sinamay swirl is made using a cardboard tube – see Chapter 9. The sinamay swirl is sewn to the headpiece using tie tacks.

The two quills can be glued together and then attached to the headpiece through this point. Once a position has been decided, a small blob of glue on the back of the quills will hold them in place while you sew them.

This shape can also be blocked on a flat brim block and the characteristic disc shape is an ideal blank canvas on which to experiment with imaginative designs.

Making a sinamay swirl.

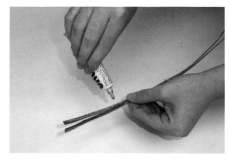

Glue the quills together.

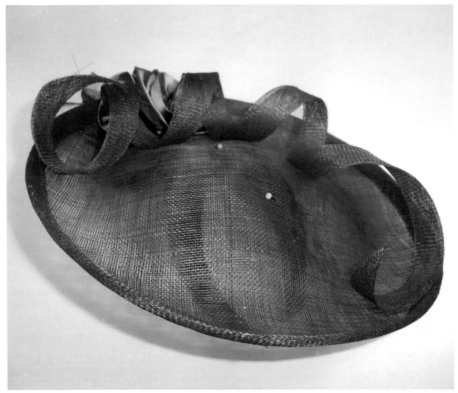

Attach the sinamay swirls to the headpiece.

Judy Bentinck Millinery. Lorelei Collection. Style: two-tone sinamay disc on a headband trimmed with hackle spray. Photographer: Alistair Cowin. Model: Emily Healey.

Judy Bentinck Millinery. Under the Rainbow Collection. Style: pink sinamay disc with lilac shot silk flowers. Photographer: Alistair Cowin. Model: Amy Macdonald.

Beth Morgan Millinery. Enchantment Collection. Style: Ripple.
Photographer: Tim Lyons. Model: Kristina Hewitt.

Justine Bradley-Hill Millinery. Style: Clara. Photography:
Ashamunn. Model: Tasha.

Freeform Sinamay Fascinator

Making the Base

Start with the fascinator base. For images of this method, refer to the turquoise sinamay fascinator, as the basic techniques are the same. Cut 21in (53cm) of cotton-covered millinery wire and curve into your preferred shape; in this case we have made it oval with a 3.5in (9cm) overlap that will go at the centre back (CB). Using Sellotape, tape the wire at the middle point to hold it together; when you're satisfied with the shape, tape both the cut ends to make sure they don't stick out.

Next, take a piece of sinamay approximately 12in (30cm) square and fold along the diagonal bias before cutting along this fold to create two triangular pieces. Spray with water and then iron so that the two pieces stick together. Lay your oval wire shape on top of the sinamay, with the overlap next to the longest straight side. This ensures that the bias runs the length of the base. Because the bias is the stretchiest part of the material with the most give, this will help when you come to shape it over the head.

Pin the wire to the sinamay using long quilter's pins to hold it in place, then cut

Freeform mauve sinamay fascinator.

**FOR THIS FASCINATOR
YOU WILL NEED:**

Scissors, thread, thimble, pins
0.5 yards (0.5m) purple sinamay
0.5 yards (0.5m) mauve sinamay
Shop-bought vintage flowers to match
Cotton-covered millinery wire
Sellotape
Water spray bottle
Elastic

around the shape, approximately 0.5in (1cm) outside the wire. Carefully push the excess sinamay over the wire using your thumbs. If it feels a little bulky, spray with a small amount of water to make it softer and easier to work with. Pin as you go. Make sure the excess turning is fairly equal all the way around. Sew using a matching thread and a quick wire stitch (*see* Chapter 4), and finish off with a secure stitch. Taking small, sharp scissors, trim the excess sinamay down to approximately 0.25in (0.5cm), making sure you don't cut into

your stitching, then iron around the outside edge.

Bind with the same colour sinamay using the method shown in Chapter 9.

ESSENTIAL SKILLS:

For this hat it may be useful to refer to Chapter 4 to find out how to sew with quick wire, back and tie tack stitches, and to Chapter 9 to learn about sinamay swirls and sinamay binding.

Making the Sculpted Freeform Shape

Take approximately half a yard (0.5m) of sinamay and fold at 90 degrees. Decide your depth – in this case, 8in (20cm). Cut across the bias width, then spray lightly with tap water. Press with a hot dry iron to give a sharp, top folded edge and also to stick the sinamay together.

Now create the shape by pleating the material with your hands and pushing it into the desired sculptural look. Pin and tack together with matching thread to make it manageable and pin in position on the base. The ends will need to be folded under or cut down.

Attaching the Freeform Shape to the Base

Pin the freeform shape to the fascinator base along the mid line, keeping the upper part of the freeform upright. Sew in place with back stitch using double thread that matches the base. Cut off any excess neatly. The selection of trims will cover all the raw edges.

Using the additional swirl trim, cover the cut edges (see Chapter 9 to learn how to make sinamay swirls). In this example, vintage pansy flowers have been sewn across the pleated edge of the freeform shape. Sew them onto the hat with matching single thread using tie tacks (as described in Chapter 4).

This fascinator is held in place on the head using elastic, which is sewn at either end of the oval base.

To the right are some more ideas for freeform headpieces, large and small.

1. Cut your wide bias strip of sinamay.

2. Pleat to create your shape and pin in position.

3. Sew in place on the base and arrange your trims.

The completed fascinator.

Judy Bentinck Millinery. Coco Rococo Collection. Style: sculpted sinamay headpiece. Photographer: Alistair Cowin. Model: Amy Macdonald.

Tracy Chaplin Millinery. Style: bronze sinamay couture headpiece. Photographer: Mark Cox.

Judy Bentinck
Millinery. Style:
large sinamay
headpiece mounted
on a wide
headband.
Photographer:
Alistair Cowin.
Model: Dagmara.

Judy Bentinck Millinery. Coco
Rococo Collection. Style: red and
gold freeform sinamay fascinator with
red peacock feathers. Photographer:
Alistair Cowin. Model: Amy
Macdonald.

Red Spot Fascinator

This is an easy-to-create little fascinator. In this example we are using a shop-bought ready-made fascinator base that will be trimmed with fabric, sinamay binding, veiling and feathers.

Taking the red and cream fabric, place over the ready-made base and pin. Next, cut to the edge of the base and sew the fabric on with a running stitch using red thread. The upper side of the base should now be covered.

Cut a bias strip of red sinamay approximately 20in (51cm) long by 2.5in (7cm) wide and create a binding as shown in Chapter 9. Sew this binding in place using slip stitch, making sure the original binding of the ready-made base has been covered and that the fabric lies smooth and flat.

Take a piece of red veiling 30in (76cm) long by 10in (26cm) deep and gather up, following the instructions for gathering in Chapter 9. Glue the feathers together and sew them to the fascinator base, then cover with the veiling, stitching it in place so that it fans out evenly across the face.

Finally, sew the hat elastic either side of the base, under the red sinamay binding.

The range of ready-made bases may be small in terms of shape and style, but there is an unlimited number of ways of using fabrics and trimmings to devise your own styles. For a few more ideas, see below:

FOR THIS FASCINATOR YOU WILL NEED:

1 ready-made ivory circular fascinator base
0.5 yards (0.5m) red sinamay
Spot fabric (enough to cover the base)
5 ivory stripped coque feathers
1 yard (1m) red Merry Widow veiling
Hat elastic
Scissors, thread, pins, needle, thimble

Red spot fascinator.

A selection of ready-made fascinator bases.

ESSENTIAL SKILLS:

For this hat it may be useful to refer to Chapter 4 to find out how to sew with slip and running/gathering stitches, and to Chapter 9 for the sinamay binding and the gathering technique.

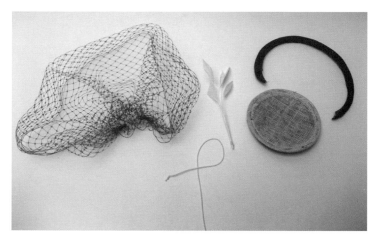

1. Your materials.

2. Cover the upper side of the fascinator base.

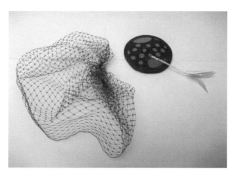

3. Bind the base.

The finished fascinator complete with elastic.

Judy Bentinck Millinery. Lorelei Collection. Style: black ready-made straw base with a peacock spray. Photographer: Alistair Cowin. Model: Emily Healey.

Judy Bentinck Millinery. Coco Rococo Collection. Style: ivory ready-made straw base with diamantes set on a headband. Photographer: Alistair Cowin. Model: Amy Macdonald.

Judy Bentinck Millinery. Coco Rococo Collection. Style: rolled sinamay covering a ready-made fascinator base. Photographer: Alistair Cowin. Model: Amy Macdonald.

N'aida Rafols Millinery. Style: hand-made fascinator covered with vintage fabrics.

Felt Fascinator

Fascinators need not necessarily be worn only in the spring and summer seasons. As well as Christmas and New Year parties, there are weddings all year round, and many other occasions when a headpiece makes a stylish addition to an outfit. Felt is more in keeping with a winter feel so here is a small, simple but stylish piece that would be suitable for a party or a wedding.

To create this felt fascinator base, join a wire to create a 14in (35cm) circle, including a 3in (7.5cm) overlap.

Lay this circle over your felt and cut the felt to the edge of the wire. Sew the two together using wire stitch. To create the binding for this piece, check that the measurement of the felt base circumference hasn't changed and add 2in (5cm) to it. The binding should not be too wide as the base is such a small shape; in this case cut a bias strip of the dupion 2in (5cm) wide by 16in (41cm) long and iron in half. Then turn in on both sides and iron to give a finished edge.

Lay one end at the centre back (CB) join and shape the silk around the wired edge, pulling gently so there are no wrinkles. At the other end fold over, turning the raw edges inside to make a

Felt fascinator.

FOR THIS FASCINATOR YOU WILL NEED:

A piece of wool felt approx 5in (13cm) squared (either left over from a previous project or cut from a wool cone)

12 × 8in (31 × 20.5cm) felt for the leaves and trim

8in rectangle of veiling

0.25 yards (0.25m) silk dupion for binding and bonding

Wire

Needle and thread, pins, thimble

Glue

small CB seam and pin in place. Stitch with matching thread using slip stitch.

Trimmings

This piece is decorated with three leaves made up of silk and felt bonded together. The directions for making these can be found in Chapter 9. We also used a small sprig of veiling. For the veiling cut an 8in (20.5cm) rectangle, gather together in the middle and secure by

wrapping matching thread around this middle area and stitching through. Place this onto the felt base and stitch.

ESSENTIAL SKILLS:

For this hat it may be useful to refer to Chapter 9 to find out how to make bonded felt leaves and fabric bindings, and to Chapter 4 for slip and wire stitches.

The bonded leaves will be attached next to the veiling, and this is then finished with a piece of hand-curled felt trim. To create this, cut a narrow length of felt either with scissors or with a sharp craft knife and simply make loops that

splay out to form a striking detail that also covers the ends of the leaves.

Hat elastic will hold this piece in place under the wearer's hair, making it easy to change the position should you wish to.

Felt is a very versatile material and the professional finished look you can achieve with it belies how easy it is to produce it. Here are some more fun ideas using the leaf shape:

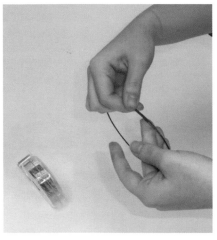

1. Join the wire to create a circle.

2. Turn in both sides of the silk dupion and iron.

3. Pin the binding in place.

4. Make the bonded leaves and attach the veiling.

5. Making the felt loops.

Judy Bentinck Millinery. Portia Collection. Style: beige felt headpiece with vintage acorns and veiling. Photographer: Alistair Cowin. Model: Lucy Shropshall.

Natasha Moorhouse Millinery. Style: Angela. Photographer: Will Strange. Model: Hanna Horn.

Judy Bentinck Millinery. Style: plum velour felt fascinator with vintage fabric and feathers.

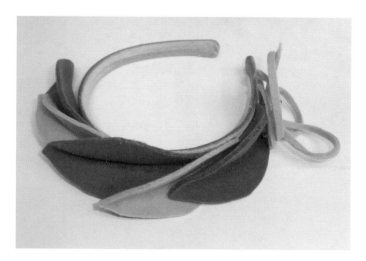

Judy Bentinck Millinery. Style: silk fabric-covered headband with pink and grey felt design.

Crin Headpiece

Crin is short for crinoline. It was originally a stiff fabric made of horsehair (it is still called horsehair in the US) and was used to help support the bottom edge of Victorian crinoline skirts. It is now made of nylon and can be bought in many different commercially dyed colours. It can also be sprayed with florist spray paint to create different effects. Be aware that too heavy a spray can leave a rather plastic-y residue on the surface and take away the delicate look that makes crin so popular. Crin photographs very effectively thanks to its sheer, lightweight sculptural qualities.

Crin comes in different widths: 6in (15cm), 5in (13cm), 3in (8cm) and 1in (2.5cm). The latter does not usually have a string running down one side, though the rest of the widths do. The string is usually triple but occasionally it is only single, so great care has to be taken when you are gathering it up. It can also be bought as a tube, with or without a lurex thread running through it. Crin can come ready pleated and sometimes printed with spots, animal patterns or diamond shapes.

To create this headpiece take a 36in (90cm) length of 6in (15cm) wide plain crin. Gently pull the string at one end

Crin headpiece.

FOR THIS HEADPIECE YOU WILL NEED:

For each flower:

35.5in (90cm) crin
Matching thread
5–7 goose biot feathers
One large hair accessory comb
Narrow ribbon

Note: You need two flowers to make this headpiece.

until you have drawn out about 12in (30cm).

Gather the cut edge of the crin into a tight bunch and wrap the string around very firmly, knotting several times. Crin frays easily so it needs to be controlled. Turn to the other end of the cut piece and again pull the string along and gather as much as you can, pushing and easing gently as you go. If the string snaps you will lose the gathered edge.

Once the crin has been gathered as

much as possible, tie off the raw end with the string, binding and knotting firmly as before.

Take this strip and, holding one

ESSENTIAL SKILLS:

For this hat it may be useful to refer to Chapter 4 to learn how to sew with tie tacks.

1. Gently pull the string from one end.

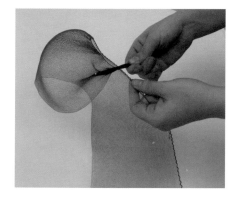

2. Tie the whole end securely.

3. Both ends tied.

4. A tulip shape.

5. Insert goose biot feathers into the centre.

6. Join the two flowers together.

7. Bind the comb with ribbon.

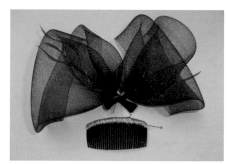

7. Bind the comb with ribbon.

8. Position the two flowers over the centre of the comb.

9. Sew the flowers in place.

gathered end, twist and turn the crin around itself, until you have created a shape you like. It can be tightly curled, which produces a tulip-shaped flower, or the outer edges can be turned down to produce an organic-looking flower, which is how this example is made. A couple of tie tacks can help to hold down the turned-over edges if needed.

For this headpiece, two crin flowers have been made with coral goose biot feathers in the middle to suggest stamens; the feathers contrast well with the navy crin, as they are a completely different texture.

Before securing the crin flower, insert your group of goose biot feathers into the middle of your flower, resting the protruding ends against the gathered end of the crin, which you should now glue to hold in place. Using the uncut crin string, wrap it around the glued feathers and the two gathered ends to join and secure the flower.

Finally, a narrow polyester ribbon is used to bind the large comb. Simply lay the end of the ribbon along the top edge of the comb and then wrap between each tooth, giving a little tug each time to make it fit closely.

End the ribbon binding approximately at the middle and start the same procedure from the other end. The two crin flowers are then positioned and pinned in place, covering the join in the middle. Sew them firmly with a double thread but don't worry if the stitches look untidy as they will be covered up. Wrap with more ribbon over the sewing and finish the ends off neatly by folding it back and stitching. There you have your finished headpiece.

Another design idea is to fan the crin out to create volume, using different length pieces to give extra depth and adding feathers and beads to give it focus. These can be mounted on a headband or a fascinator base with a comb. They are light and easy to wear and look very chic.

Beth Morgan Millinery. Style: Milkyway (blue crin with Swarovski crystals). Photographer: Archibald Photography. Model: Pamela Mckillop.

Judy Bentinck Millinery. Coco Rococo Collection. Style: looped narrow crin with coque feathers on a headband. Photographer: Alistair Cowin. Model: Amy Macdonald.

Judy Bentinck Millinery. Lorelei Collection. Style: wide black crin headpiece trimmed with olive goose and natural guinea-fowl feathers. Photographer: Alistair Cowin. Model: Emily Healey.

Mandy McGregor Millinery. Style: black crin headpiece.

Bridal Fascinator

There is a huge demand for bridal fascinators, headpieces, veils and tiaras. You only have to look at the number of wedding fairs and wedding shops to see the wide range of styles available for that 'Very Important Day'. Here we have a pretty, lace-covered base, trimmed with delicate feathers and lace flowers. Veiling could be added, as indeed could beads or diamantes or maybe flowers to tie in with the bouquet.

Making the Base

The following method is different from the other fascinator bases described here because this piece is covered in lace so it is unnecessary to have the sinamay covering the wire. Cut 17in (43cm) of white wire, curve it into an oval shape with your thumb and tape the overlapping ends. The middle of the overlap of the wire will be the centre back (CB).

Take two pieces of ivory sinamay 6in (15cm) square and iron together. Next, place the wire over the sinamay so the bias runs along the length of the base. Mark around the outside of the wire with a marker pencil, pin in the middle of the sinamay to hold the layers together and cut along this line.

Now, starting at the CB, sew the wire

Ivory lace bridal fascinator.

FOR THIS FASCINATOR YOU WILL NEED:

Scissors, thread, thimble, pins, needle

0.5 yard (0.5m) ivory sinamay

0.25 yard (0.25m) ivory lace

Bondaweb

Ivory petersham

Ivory hackle feathers

Cotton-covered millinery wire

to the edge of the sinamay using wire stitch and matching thread. There will be no excess sinamay.

Now cut a piece of ivory lace which is bigger by 0.5in (1cm) than the wired base. Lay this over the sinamay with the edge folded in and sewn with a running stitch resting next to the edge of the wire. Use ivory thread so the stitches don't show. Make sure the lace lies smooth over the base and trim any excess away from the wired edge.

ESSENTIAL SKILLS:

For this hat it may be useful to refer to Chapter 4 to learn how to make a petersham binding and for the running, tacking, stab and wire stitches, and to Chapter 9 for bonded lace flowers.

1. Join the wire with Sellotape.

3. Sew the wire to the edge of the sinamay.

Binding with Petersham

The base is bound with ivory petersham, which has been made into a loop to fit (see Chapter 4). Loop the petersham over the wire, lining up the CBs. Pin in place and then tack (baste) around with a contrasting thread.

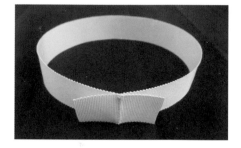

1. The petersham loop for binding.

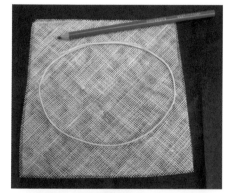

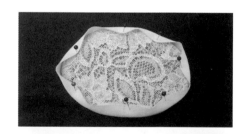

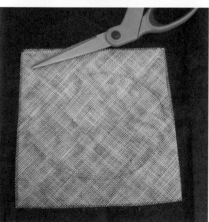

2. Mark around the wire and cut out.

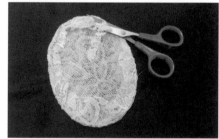

2. Pin in place and tack.

4. Sew the lace next to the wire and trim the excess off.

3. Shrink to fit.

Take the pins out. Dampen a clean and soft absorbent cloth and wipe it evenly around the petersham. It will then shrink to fit. If any areas remain a little bumpy, just smooth them with your fingers until they disappear. Leave the petersham to dry and then stitch with stab stitch with matching thread. Remove the tacking.

1. Iron the bondaweb sticky side down and cut away the excess.

Making the Trimming

Next, create the trim with the bonded lace flowers and ivory hackle feathers. These pretty flowers are made of floral lace, from which you cut out each flower shape. Find two flowers that match and cut a small square of Bondaweb to fit. Iron the Bondaweb with the sticky side down on one side of one lace flower. You will be ironing the paper side. Cut the excess Bondaweb away. Remove the paper backing and place the opposing lace flower on top, matching carefully.

Iron again, but this time place a soft cloth between the iron and the lace (to prevent any stickiness coming through the lace onto your iron). The two flowers will now be bonded together. They are then given a little stitched pleat at the bottom, which will make them stand up a little and give them a bit of extra

2. Place the opposing flower on top.

interest. Repeat to create another flower.

Take a small group of ivory hackle feathers and glue them together to create the fanned-out shape. Wrap a piece of ivory cotton around the glue to hold the feathers in the desired shape and put to one side to dry.

Arrange the two groups of feathers at the CB, radiating out over the base. Attach the two lace flowers decoratively over the join between the two groups of feathers.

To finish this bridal headpiece, it can be set on a comb with or without hat elastic depending on the bride's hair and what hairstyle is chosen.

There is a huge market for bridal headpieces, and designs can include veils, beading, vintage trims, pearls, diamante, matching wedding dress fabric and much more. For some more ideas for that special day, see over page:

Now you have learned how to create a variety of headpieces, the following chapter covers the basics of cut and sewn hats.

Give the flower lift with a stitched pleat.

Glue the feathers together and wrap with thread.

Arrange the feathers and flowers over the base.

Beth Morgan Millinery. Enchantment Collection. Style: Glitz full face veil. Photographer: Tim Lyons. Model: Kristina Hewitt.

Judy Bentinck Millinery. Coco Rococo Collection. Style: ivory crin fascinator with diamantes and aqua quills. Photographer: Alistair Cowin. Model: Amy Macdonald.

Beth Morgan Millinery. Eternity Collection. Style: 'Jellyfish', large crin headpiece with double-sided satin ribbon rosette. Photographer: Archibald Photography. Model: Pamela Mckillop.

Chapter 8
Cut and Sewn Hats

8

Cut and sewn hats essentially use dressmaking techniques. Rather than using specific millinery materials such as straws and felts, they are made by creating a paper pattern, cutting it out in fabric and then sewing it together using a domestic sewing machine. The simplest cut and sewn hat is the mob-cap, most notably worn in the Victorian era by household servants or as a bathing cap. Even earlier it was worn perched atop an enormous wig, as was the fashion in Georgian times. The mob-cap is a circle of fabric gathered up to create a frilly edge and a big puffed area which can cover the hair either partially or completely, or it can be used to decorative effect, not really covering the hair at all, as was the preference among the Georgians. Essentially the cap was worn by servants to keep their hair free from dust and dirt and by bathers to keep their hair dry – as indeed they do now with the same design being used in modern shower caps.

Another very simple style of unstructured hat is made using a rectangular headscarf. Queen Elizabeth II has always championed this type of headwear, wearing it in the traditional way tied under the chin. It keeps you warm and stops your hair from being affected by the weather. The headscarf was at its most popular during the 1940s when, out of necessity caused by the austerity of wartime, women were extremely inventive with their styling.

More and more women were also working outside of the home, often in factories, and the headscarf tied up as a turban was a perfect way to keep their hair out of machinery or harm's way.

In this chapter we cover two simple styles of cut and sewn hat: the beret and the bandeau.

A 1940s-style headscarf tied as a turban. Photograph: Judy Bentinck. Model: Freya Berry.

Fabric beret.

Silk fabric bandeau.

LEFT: Judy Bentinck Millinery. Style: fabric beret. Photographer: Alistair Cowin. Model: Tamlyn Williams. Make-up and hair: Sammy Carpenter.

Fabric Beret

The first example of a cut and sewn hat is a standard beret pattern, which can be adapted to create a variety of styles. A beret is a soft, round hat with a flat crown that can be worn in different ways, either by shaping it with the hands or by creating different looks by pulling it to one side, wearing it straight, pulling it forward or having it pushed to the back of the head. It can be worn by both men and women and has an extremely long history. Beret-style hats arguably date back to as early as the Bronze Age and throughout history they have typically been worn by French men, the Spanish (particularly in the Basque country) and in Scotland, where it is known as the tam-o'shanter and features a large pompom in the centre. It is typically used in military uniforms and became iconic when worn by Che Guevara in the 1960s. Most styles of beret are made from wool with the headband often made out of leather. Traditionally, the beret would be turned inwards along the edge so that the headband was worn on the inside and it often had a means of tightening with a drawstring. Another strong symbolic version of the beret is the Rastafarian Kufi. This knitted or crocheted hat is big enough to accommodate long

Wool fabric beret with organdie poppies.

FOR THIS HAT YOU WILL NEED:

Scissors, pins, thimble and needle
1 yard (1m) wool fabric (in this example lightweight wool)
0.5 yards (0.5m) lining fabric (polyester or silk)
Sewing thread
Sewing machine

For the poppies:
0.5 yards (0.5m) organdie
Sinamay
Sewing thread

dreadlocks and is decorated with red, green and orange.

This particular beret pattern has a quite wide soft band that fits around the head and is on show as part of the design. It is full and floppy, and can be styled in several ways. It has a lining that covers the internal sewing, giving it a lovely finish and adding warmth for the wearer, particularly if it is silk rather than polyester. This beret has been styled with two poppies for decoration but you could also use feathers, a smaller flower or a lightweight brooch as alternatives.

For this design, high-quality, lightweight wool fabric has been used to give the floppy effect that is characteristic of this style of beret. Polyester was used for the

ESSENTIAL SKILLS:

For this hat it may be useful to refer to Chapter 4 to learn how to take a head measurement and sew with running and slip stitches, and to Chapter 9 for the poppy patterns and instructions.

What your paper pattern will look like.

1. Joining the crown and under crown.

2. Machine sew the centre back seam of the head band.

3. Join the headband to the underbrim. Remember that the right sides of the fabric face one another.

4. Pin the lining into the beret.

5. Sew with a running stitch.

6. Fold down the raw edge of the band.

7. Fold it in half.

8. Pin to cover the lining and hand sew.

The finished (undecorated) beret.

lining. Silk, though more expensive, would make the hat warmer to wear.

Using brown parcel paper, draw 2 circles 13in (33cm) across (giving a 6.5in/17cm radius) using a compass, or draw around a plate or biscuit tin if the dimensions are correct. One circle will be the crown and the other the under brim. Next, draw a long rectangle 4in (10cm) deep and 24in (61cm) long. This is the band that goes around the head, so the seam allowance will vary according to the person's head measurement. For example, if the head size is 22in (56cm), using a 24in (61cm) long rectangle will give you a 2in (5cm) back seam allowance. To find the correct length, take the head measurement as shown in Chapter 4 and add 2in (5cm) to allow for the seam.

On the second circle pattern draw a smaller circle 6in (16cm) across (giving a 3in/8cm radius) and cut this out. This will create the head opening (known as the headfitting). Mark each circle with centre back (CB), centre front (CF) and both sides at 3 and 9 o'clock. This pattern piece will be the under crown. On the band, mark the seam allowance and also half the depth. This will be the halfway turning mark when you sew the headband into the lining, hiding any raw edges.

Cut out these three pattern pieces

carefully. Lay the paper pattern onto the fabric and pin, ensuring there are no creases in the pattern. Cut out using good-quality dressmaking scissors. Remove the paper pattern but make sure you know where the CB is. Join the crown and the under crown pieces and pin the circles together with pins facing inwards so it is easy to sew through the middle of them.

Sew the two circles together with a 0.5in (1cm) seam allowance using a sewing machine and reverse stitch to prevent your stitching coming undone. Clip every 1in (3cm) so the seam is less bulky.

Take your pattern again and cut the two circles in your lining material, marking up as you did before. Sew the two pieces of lining fabric together with the sewing machine.

Make up the headband to the required length and pin it to the opening in your under crown, starting with the CB seam and pinning along the seam allowance. When the headband has been sewn to the underbrim and clipped, press the CB seam open and then turn the hat right side out.

Sit the lining inside the beret, matching the seam all the way round. Pin at the seam allowance of the band (the headfitting). Sew with a hand running stitch to secure.

Next, fold down the raw edge of the band 1in (2cm) and fold again in half. Pin this folded edge to the hat's headfitting, hiding the seams. Hand hem the turned edge using slip stitch. Iron the band with a damp cloth between the fabric and the iron. This will give a perfect finish.

Decorate with two poppies (*see* Chapter 9).

Silk Fabric Bandeau

Using a yard (1m) of silk dupion (right sides facing), find the true bias by folding the fabric at 45 degrees using the selvedge as a guide. Iron and cut along this fold. Cut a band 10in (26cm) deep. In this example it is 40in (102cm) long. Fold in half lengthways, mark the centre back (CB) and cut the ends into matching points. Machine around the three open sides with a 0.5in (1cm) seam allowance, leaving a gap on the bottom straight edge approximately 5in (13cm) long at the CB mark.

Trim off the seam allowance at the points so there is as little fabric as possible. The points should lie flat and look sharp when they have been turned. Turn the whole piece inside out and use the point turner tool (if you have one) to make the points sharp. This can also be done with small scissors.

Hand sew the gap with a small slip stitch and then iron the whole piece. Fold in half, creating a CB mark. Next, create the centre front (CF) detail. From the CB, measure half the required head measurement (e.g 11in/28cm if you have a 22in head size) and mark this on both halves. Run a gathering stitch vertically on both sides, drawing up the fabric to create a ruffled effect.

Using a wooden or polystyrene dolly, wrap the bandeau around the headfitting area with the gathers at the CF. Overlap the two loose ends and twist

Silk dupion bandeau.

them around themselves to form a knot. Sew through the middle to keep the knot in place. Pin the pointed ends in place and stitch using a tie tack under the fabric. Voilà: a chic bandeau!

Silk lends itself very well to an elegant look for an evening occasion. A patterned cotton would be ideal for a summer's day.

Other cut and sewn hats using flat patterns are the classic flat cap or a sectioned fabric rain hat or sun hat. Caps for men or women, or toques (small brimless hats), are also made this way. Here are some more examples of some

very stylish cut and sewn hats.

By now, you will have learnt many different ways of making hats and headpieces and next you will be introduced to some exciting ways of trimming them.

FOR THIS BANDEAU YOU WILL NEED:

1 yard (1m) silk dupion (or fabric of your choice)
Scissors, needle, pins, thimble
Matching thread
Sewing machine
Polystyrene dolly head
Point turner tool

ESSENTIAL SKILLS:

For this hat it may be useful to refer to Chapter 4 to find out how to sew with slip, gathering and tie tack stitches.

1. Leave a 5in gap in the middle of the cut edge.

2. Create neat points.

4. Pull the stitching to create the gathers.

3. Mark where you will gather.

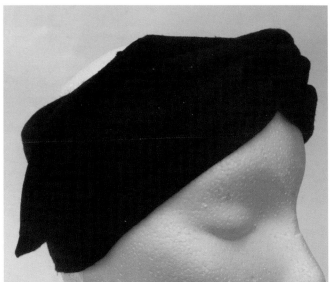

5. The finished bandeau.

An example of a bandeau made from sinamay. Judy Bentinck Millinery. Under the Rainbow Collection. Photographer: Alistair Cowin. Model: Amy Macdonald. Make-up and hair: Ruth Hancox.

Karen Henriksen Millinery. Showtime Collection. Style: Sarah.

Karen Henriksen Millinery. Showtime Collection. Style: Mitzi.

Karen Henriksen Millinery. Girl Racer Collection. Style: Jenson/Dashing. Photographer: Tim Scott, Fluid Images. Model: Danni Menzies. Make-up and hair: Polly Mann.

Chapter 9
Trimmings

The world-renowned teacher Rose Cory commented that 'trimmings on hats should look as if they have just fallen from the sky', meaning that their placement shouldn't be overworked or look too heavy on the hat. Rose was milliner to the Queen Mother for forty years and is a Royal Warrant Holder so she sets a good example for the rest of us to follow.

Bows

Fabric bow

You will need a yard (1m) of shot silk or a fabric of your choice. To start, iron the fabric smooth. Then cut four rectangular fabric strips on the bias measuring 5 × 10in (13 × 26cm) and arrange in pairs, placing one on top of the other. Also cut a single piece of fabric on the bias 5 × 4in (13 × 10cm); this will be used later.

1. Place the rectangles into pairs and join.

Using a sewing machine, sew the long sides of the double rectangle, with right sides together, thus creating a tube. Turn the tube inside out and press the top and bottom edges. At the cut ends make a tuck or pleat. Sew by hand. This keeps the fabric under control. Fold in half and sew the pleated ends together to form the bow shape.

2. Turn the right sides out to form a tube.

3. Pleat the bottom edge and sew.

4. Sew the pleated ends together.

Take the single piece of fabric and from it form a small tuck; hold this at the centre back of the bow. Fold the outside raw edges in and drape around the middle part of the bow. Pin into the back of the bow and sew.

5. Sew the middle section at the back of the bow.

Tweak the fabric to puff it out a little. This bow can be seen used as a trim on the brown felt cloche that features as an example at the end of the wool felt cloche hat.

LEFT: Judy Bentinck Millinery. Style: mauve freeform sinamay fascinator. Photographer: Alistair Cowin. Model: Tamlyn Williams. Make-up and hair: Sammy Carpenter.

Sinamay Bow

Take a strip of sinamay across the bias and cut to 6.5 × 24in (17 × 61cm). Stretch out both ways. Fold the top cut edge down by 1.5in (4cm) and press with your fingers along the length of the top edge. Fold up the other side 2in (5cm) and repeat.

1. Fold the top edge down and press.

2. Repeat on the other side.

Cut the length in half and fold each piece in half. Pleat each one in the same direction. Hand sew to secure. Overlap and sew together.

3. Fold in half and pleat.

4. Sew together.

Cut another strip to 5.5 × 4.5in (14 × 12cm), which will wrap around the middle section of the bow, and fold in the cut edges as before. Pleat both ends and wrap this around the middle of the bow and sew at the back.

5. Fold in the cut edges of your middle section.

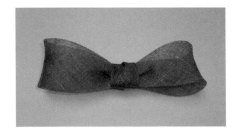

6. Wrap the sinamay around the middle and sew.

Organdie Bow

You will need 30in (75cm) of cotton organdie in a colour of your choice. Place the fabric on the bias and cut a strip 28in (71cm) along the top edge, 20in (51cm) along the bottom and 4.5in (12cm) deep. Press with a steam iron to remove any creases. Fold in half and cut both points off 1.5in (4cm) into the straight edge. Cut one single rectangle 3in (8cm) wide. The remaining piece is the main part of the bow.

1. Cut the points off.

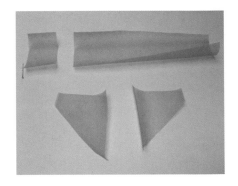

2. Pieces cut as required.

Taking the main piece, roll along both long edges, rolling away from you and pulling sideways to keep it crisp. Fold both ends into the middle and, with a small running stitch, gather in to form a bow. Roll the edges of the pointed pieces, leaving the top edge unrolled. Make sure each piece faces away from the other to suggest the ties of the bow.

Roll the remaining narrow piece and wrap around the middle of the bow (the

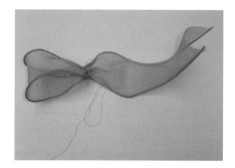

3. Start to form the bow.

4. Roll the edges of the pointed pieces and place in position.

gathered part) – this will need cutting down to fit. Pin. Add the 'ties' to the centre back and sew, making sure the stitches can't be seen at the front.

5. The finished bow.

Simple Petersham Bow

This is a traditional bow used on both men's and women's hats. It is particularly suitable for styles such as the trilby, fedora or a simple cloche. The bow sits on the left side for men and on the right for women.

Cut two pieces of petersham, one 6in (15cm) and the other 8in (20cm) long. Mitre or fishtail the ends of the shorter piece. Taking the longer piece, make it into a loop and oversew together with matching thread. Next, place the looped piece on top of the mitred or fishtailed shorter piece, lining up the centres.

1. Place the loop on the mitred or fishtailed piece.

Sew together along the centre line with a running stitch, again in matching thread. Next, cut a third piece of matching petersham 3in (8cm) long and wrap around the middle section, joining the cut edges with a running stitch. This section should fit neatly around the bow. The bow will then lie flat against the headband.

2. The finished bows.

If petersham is being used as a hatband to accompany the bow, it needs to be curved with a hot steam iron to shrink the top edge to lie flat against the shape of the crown.

Felt

Working with Felt

You can use leftover felt to create a variety of effective bows, leaves, flowers and loops for hats and fascinators. Before creating your trims, you may need to flatten out any 'frillyness' resulting from the blocking process by using a wet cloth and a hot iron. In sections, lay the wet cloth onto the felt and press with the iron on the hottest setting (usually the linen setting) for ten seconds.

1. An example of leftover blocked felt.

2. Press with a wet cloth and hot iron.

Remove and then pull the felt both ways, which will straighten it out and remove the wavy shapes. For long pieces of trim do this all along the felt. If you are only creating a couple of small shapes (like leaves for example), then 6–8in (15–20cm) should be enough.

When cutting felt, you can cut freehand with scissors to your chosen

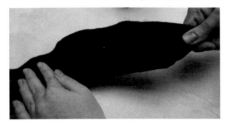

3. Pull the felt both ways.

4. Cutting with scissors.

width for a long trim, or use a craft knife on a cutting board for a more precise finish.

To curl felt, paint a little felt stiffener on one side, leave to dry and then wrap around a tube and steam, turning the tube for an even finish.

Alternatively merely loop the felt into your desired shape. This is how to make the trim to go with the Wool Felt Cloche.

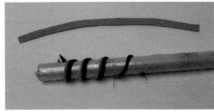

5. Wrapping felt around a tube.

Felt Leaves

Flatten out your felt as above (if necessary). Using the medium-sized leaf pattern shown here, pin the pattern onto the felt and cut out. Fold the leaf in half lengthways and cover with a wet cloth.

Press for ten seconds with a hot iron. This makes it warm and moist so it is easy to pull and stretch with your hands to make the leaf more natural looking, with a little life and twist to it.

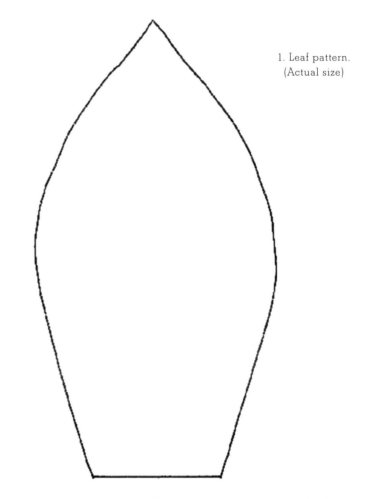

1. Leaf pattern. (Actual size)

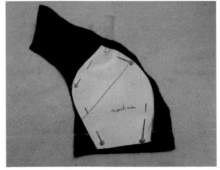

2. Pin and cut around your pattern.

3. Fold the leaf in half.

4. Pull and stretch the shape with your hands.

5. A leaf with a pleat at the base.

Veiling

Veiling is generally made of nylon these days, although vintage silk veiling may still be available – at a price. It is sometimes referred to as netting but should be called veiling as that is its purpose. Veiling comes in different colours and widths, with and without removable chenille spots. These are sometimes called spot veiling and merry widow veiling respectively.

Full Face Veiling

Measure and cut a 36in (90cm) length, gather both ends and secure with a few stitches.

Run a single thread along the top edge to gather. The depth of this is decided by the design – in this case, it is two squares down from the top edge. With a long thread knotted at the end, insert the needle through the sewn, gathered end of the veiling and weave the needle in and out of each diamond-

Bonded Leaves

In the felt fascinator project, three of these leaves feature as decoration. They are created using felt bonded to another fabric to produce an interesting double-sided finish; in this example, silk dupion has been used. Cut the leaf out in both felt and your chosen fabric using the paper pattern.

1. Felt and silk dupion bonded leaves.

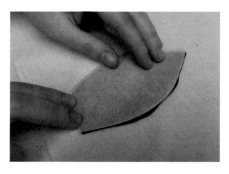

2. Place the Bondaweb glued side down.

3. Peel off the backing paper.

Cut a piece of Bondaweb approximately the same size as the felt and place it glued side down. Iron with a hot iron on the paper side until it sticks to the felt. Cut to fit and then peel off the paper backing. Iron the dupion to this glued side.

The leaf shape can now be manipulated to look more leaf-like using the method above.

4. Iron the dupion to the sticky side.

5. The first finished leaf on the felt fascinator.

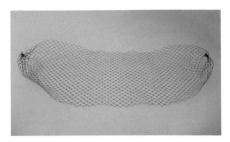

1. Gather the ends of the veiling.

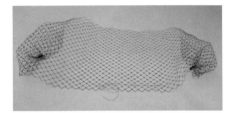

2. Weave the thread in and out of each diamond to create gathers.

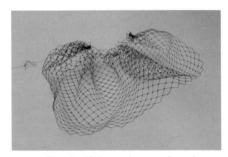

3. Finish off the gathering thread.

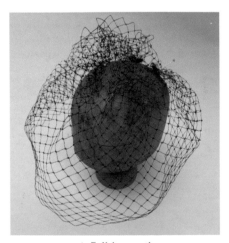

4. Full face veil.

shaped gap.

At the other end, leave the needle and thread attached, then gently gather the veiling along the thread, arranging it to suit the hat or headpiece to make sure there is plenty of space between it and the wearer's face, especially the nose and eyelashes. When the position has been decided, finish off the thread by sewing into the other gathered end and cut.

The veiling is then attached at a few points to hold it in place. Tie tacks are the best stitch to use. The cut ends of the gathered veiling can be hidden with a suitable trim. This method was used for the parisial pillbox hat. *See* Chapter 4 for an explanation of tie tacks.

Birdcage Veil

This is an American style that has become popular in the UK. It is a short veil, usually only reaching to just beneath the nose. It is easier to wear than the full face veil and goes well with the 1950s style of dress, particularly mounted on a fascinator or headpiece. This is very popular with those who favour the 'Rockabilly' look.

Cut 32in (80cm) of 6in (15cm) deep veiling and follow the same method as

Red Spot fascinator.

for the full face veil. This particular veil has been set on a sinamay fascinator base that has been covered with fabric.

Veiling Detail

Veiling can also be used to good effect as a detail. For example, cut a 7in (18cm) by 10in (25cm) rectangle and halfway along gather together and sew firmly. This trimming can then be used for covering up the ends of feathers or stitching by positioning it in a suitable place using tie tacks (*see* Chapter 4). Veiling detail also adds height to a piece.

Felt fascinator.

Sinamay Trimmings

Sinamay Swirls

This is a very useful trimming technique. Take a bias strip of ready-stiffened sinamay. Fold in half and iron, before opening up again to turn both sides into the middle and iron again. Lastly, iron

Sinamay rolled on a cardboard tube.

the two sides together to ensure no raw edges are showing. If at any point the sinamay isn't sticking together, spray it with a little tap water. The strip can then be manipulated into bows or loops, or bound around a cardboard tube and steamed. It can then be cut and arranged on a hat or a headpiece – the choice is yours. The cardboard tube method is used in the trimming on the sinamay picture hat.

1. Spray with tap water.

2. This double loop is formed by hand.

3. Remove any excess sinamay.

Ironed Sinamay Detail

Take a bias strip of ready-stiffened sinamay approximately 9in (23cm) long. The width can vary according to your design but always bear in mind it needs to be 2in (5cm) wider than the finished piece. Turn the top edge in 0.5in (1.25cm), matching the grains all along, and iron. Fold this over again and iron again; this produces a clean sharp detail. Repeat on the bottom edge. If there is any resistance, simply spray it with a little tap water.

Once prepared, the sinamy strip can be looped or pleated, or steamed on a cardboard tube to create interesting shapes.

To finish the cut ends, fold over twice and iron flat, cutting off the excess.

The density of the ironed edge contrasts well with the delicate single layer in the middle. This is the method used to create the turquoise sinamay fascinator.

Rolled Sinamay Detail

This is a lovely way to finish the raw edges of sinamay and looks very effective. Cut a bias strip of ready-stiffened sinamay approximately 5in (13cm) wide. Spray gently with water and leave it for a few moments to become tacky. Starting on the right-hand end, use both hands to roll the sinamay away from you with the pads of your forefingers over the pads of your thumbs. Be sure to roll quite tightly so that it doesn't come undone.

Next, pull both ways to tighten and firm the roll. Continue all the way along, ensuring that you have a neat and even rolled edge along the required length.

To create the finished point, continue to roll as you meet the straight grain, curving the sinamay as you move towards the end. Repeat the whole process along the bottom edge and then apply a tiny amount of UHU glue to the

very end and leave it to dry. Cut to create a sharp point. You can then manipulate this in a variety of ways.

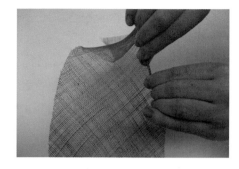

1. Rolling the sinamay.

2. Roll along the length to the pointed ends.

3. Rolling the sinamay on the bias gives a professional look.

Sinamay Binding

To create the binding, use the same method as demonstrated in sinamay swirls, but without curling it. To use this trim as a binding, you need to either steam or spray with water to soften it and make it easy to curve around your brim or fascinator base as shown in the turquoise sinamay fascinator, pinning in place and ending with a small, vertical centre back seam. Any bumps or distortions can be pressed out with your fingers as you go or ironed away. Pin, then stitch this in place with a slip stitch and matching thread so the sewing cannot be seen.

Curve the binding around the wire and pin.

Parisisal Twirls

Take a length of parisisal approx 2.5in (6.5cm) wide, spray with water on both sides and fold in the top edge and press with a hot iron. Then fold the other side in to slightly overlap with the opposite fold. Press firmly with a hot iron.

Pin onto a cardboard tube and turn around the tube, pushing gently with your thumb. Cut the ends at a 45 degree angle to give a finished look and glue the open ends shut with a small amount of UHU glue. Sew in position on your hat or headpiece with tie tacks.

1. Fold in both sides and press with a hot iron.

2. Pin onto a cardboard tube.

3. Cut the ends at a 45 degree angle.

Flowers

Sinamay Stamens

Cut a rectangle of sinamay on the straight grain and dampen to soften the sinamay. Remove the weft, leaving only the warp threads with 0.5in (1cm) area at the bottom unshredded. Roll this up and stitch with a secure running stitch.

You can also buy ready-made stamens from specialist flower suppliers and online.

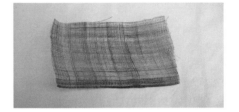

1. Cut a rectangle of sinamay.

2. Remove the weft.

3. Stitch at the base.

Poppies

We have used cotton organdie for this flower as it has a unique crispness that lends itself well to the look and feel of a poppy flower petal. Two of these poppies have been used to decorate the fabric beret.

Using the two poppy petal patterns, cut out four large poppy petals and four small poppy petals on the bias. Match the grain line on the pattern to the grain on the fabric.

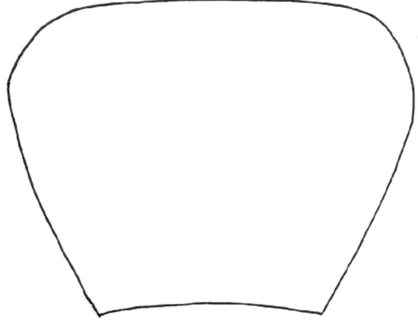

1. Poppy pattern. (Actual size)

2. Cut out the petals.

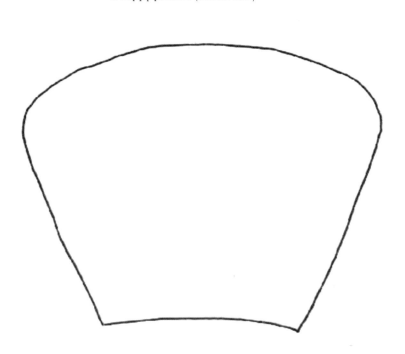

3. Fold the petal in half and place on damp fabric.

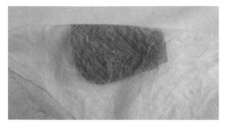

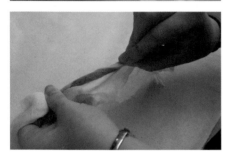

4. Make the poppy petals by rolling and twisting.

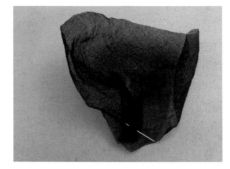

5. Pinning a pleat.

6. Sew the stamen in place.

7. Sew the second petal opposite the first.

8. Continue placing petals on opposing sides until your poppy takes shape.

Taking each petal in turn, fold it in half and place on the bias of a piece of fine clean damp fabric – muslin is perfect, but a J-cloth can also be used. Using the bias of the fabric will make it easier to roll and crease.

Fold the damp fabric over the petal and then roll it. Next twist it as if you were wringing it out. Carefully unroll the cloth, take off the petal from the cloth and leave to dry. Before each petal is completely dry, open it out and pull gently across the bias, as this curls it and gives it a poppy-like shape. Leave to dry fully.

Repeat for all eight petals. To make up the finished poppy, start with one of the small poppy petals, pleat it in at the bottom edge and pin.

Next place the pleat against the bottom of a rolled stamen (*see* above) and sew with stab stitch (*see* Chapter 4).

Place the second small petal on the opposite side of the stamen and sew in place.

The next two petals are attached on the opposing sides. Do the same on the outside with the larger petals. Lastly, arrange the petals and stamens into the desired shape.

Boat Flowers

These are also known as 'U' or 'bias' flowers and this is a very simple but effective technique for creating flowers from fabric. The word 'boat' describes the cut shape of the fabric used to create each flower. The fabric is cut on the bias and can be any depth, but the flowers made to trim the blocked sinamay headpiece have been made in three sizes: two at 16 × 2in (41 × 4cm), one at 32 × 3in (82 × 8cm) and the last at 26 × 3in (66 × 8cm). To create these flowers, cut two bias strips of 16 × 4in (41 × 8cm), one bias strip of 32 × 6in (88 × 16cm) and another bias strip of 26 × 6in (66 × 16cm).

Fold each strip in half along the long length of the silk dupion and cut the ends to form a curve, thus producing a long, shallow boat shape.

Using matching single thread with a knot at the end, start sewing with a running stitch from the top edge about 0.25in (0.5cm) from the cut edge. Sew all the way along and leave the thread

1. Fold in half lengthways and cut.

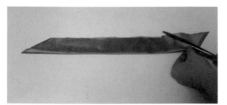

2. Sew with a single thread.

3. Gather up.

4. Sew the bottom edge.

5. Arrange your boat flowers to suit the design of your hat or headpiece.

free at the other end. Carefully gather all the way along the running stitch-line.

To make the fabric into a flower shape, pull the pointed end down to the bottom edge. Wrap the gathered edge around itself, making sure that the cut edge is at the same level throughout. Once you have created a flower shape you're happy with, pin in place. Sew firmly through the bottom gathered edge, making sure that no cut edges poke through the middle of the flower on the top.

Bonded Lace Flowers

Because lace comes in many colours and floral designs, sometimes beaded or corded, it is a great source for potential trims. To make these bonded flowers,

find two flowers on your chosen lace that match and cut them out. Cut a small square of Bondaweb to fit and iron the Bondaweb with the sticky side down on one side of the lace flower. You will be ironing the paper side. Then cut away the excess Bondaweb.

Remove the paper backing and place the opposing lace on top, matching carefully. Iron again but this time with a soft cloth between the iron and the lace (to prevent the stickiness coming through the lace onto your iron). The two flowers will now be bonded together.

1. Place Bondaweb sticky side down, press with an iron and cut away any excess.

2. Put the opposing lace on top.

These flowers are then given a little stitched pleat at the bottom which will make them stand up a little and give them a bit of extra interest. Repeat to create as many flowers as you need for your particular trim. You can see this technique put into practise in the bridal fascinator.

Feathers

Feathers are a traditional hat accessory and there is a huge variety to choose from, giving you an abundance of trimming options from the demure to the flamboyant. Some specialist feather companies are listed in the Suppliers List at the back of the book. The hats in this book feature trimmings made from quills, goose biots, coque feathers, hackle feathers and guinea-fowl feathers.

Quills are the stripped spines of ostrich feathers. They are sometimes referred to as spines or spadonas (the latter meaning a type of sword). Quills have been used on the sinamay picture hat and the blocked sinamay headpiece. They come in a wide variety of commercially dyed colours but they can also be hand-coloured using florist's spray paint. Quills can be cut to different lengths and curled, using heated curling tongs or the back of a pair of scissors (in the same way that you would curl ribbons for gift-wrapping). The top third of a quill is the most flexible part; beyond that it may kink or bend.

Biots are the single fibres from the large wing feathers of a goose. They have a distinctive look and hold their shape well but can also be curled using the same technique as the quill above,

creating a spiral. In the crin headpiece, a small group of biots were joined together to create the effect of stamens.

Other commonly used feathers are those from cockerels, known as coq or coque feathers (pronounced 'coke' in the UK). These feathers are used in the turquoise sinamay fascinator and the red spot fascinator. Hackle feathers come from the neck of male and female chickens and are very light and delicate. They have been used with bonded lace flowers to create a graceful trim in the bridal fascinator.

Lastly, guinea-fowl feathers come in a range of commercially dyed colours as well as their natural black and white plumage. They can look very effective and have been used to make the feather flower in the turquoise sinamay fascinator.

Clockwise from left: pack of dyed guinea-fowl feathers, a collection of coloured quills, a fan of stripped coque, guinea-fowl feathers on a fringe, three colours of goose biots on a fringe.

Vintage Trimmings

There is a wealth of beautiful vintage items to be found, such as buttons, brooches, lace, fabric flowers and feathers, which make unique and effective trimmings. Second-hand shops, thrift stores and antique markets can be an Aladdin's cave of distinctive ideas and there are also many haberdashery and vintage sites online to search for that perfect finishing touch.

Fabric trims such as felt, velvet, silk, cotton and synthetic fibres can be revived by steaming or ironing. Straws such as sinamay and parisisal can also benefit from this. Another useful tip is to spray with a solution of diluted laundry starch or corn starch. This gives the fabric a newly sharp, crisp feel. Veiling can also be refreshed by using a cool iron, and tired feathers can be given a new lease of life by holding them in the steam of a kettle, making sure you don't hold the feather too close to the spout.

Many milliners take advantage of the unique and quirky edge that antique embellishments give their designs, playfully exploring the possibilities of unusual items such as watch cogs, buckles, hat pins, costume jewellery and coins. The possibilities are endless.

Shop-bought flowers.

Sheena Holland. Style: Princess Butler Tiara (handmade sequined velvet headband mounted with marcasite diamante and pearls with vintage glass and early plastic jewellery).

Glossary

Abaca: Fibre from a species of banana tree used in the production of sinamay.

Bandeau: Material draped around the head without covering the crown.

Beret: A soft cap with a circular crown.

Bias: The cross grain of a woven material.

Binding: Covering the outer edge of a base or brim.

Block: A wooden or buckram mould used to shape hats.

Blocking: The description of the act of moulding a hat shape on a block.

Bondaweb: A fusible fabric used to join two layers together.

Brim: Part of the hat that extends beyond the crown.

Buckram: Canvas-like material treated with glue.

Capeline: A large brimmed hood used for blocking.

Catching: Sewing through a fabric with shallow stitches.

CB: Centre back.

CF: Centre front.

Clip: Small cuts made to make material lie smooth, particularly along a curve.

Cloche: Close-fitting hat with a round crown and a small brim.

Cocktail hat: A small brimless hat.

Cone: Similar to capeline, but smaller and conically shaped.

Couture: High quality.

Crin: A nylon woven fabric, originally made from horsehair.

Crown: Top of the hat that covers the head.

Cut and sewn: Hats made from a pattern and sewn with a machine.

Dolly head: A polystyrene or wooden head used to display hats.

Domette: Soft interfacing.

Fitting: Trying on a hat to see if it suits.

Fusible: Sticks together.

Grain: The warp and weft of a material.

Grosgrain: Ribbed ribbon.

Hatter: Maker of men's hats.

Headfitting: Size of a hat by head measurement.

Headribbon: Petersham ribbon attached to the inside of the headfitting.

Hood: Refers to a cone or capeline.

Interfacing: Extra layer of material used for strengthening.

Milliner: Maker of women's hats.

Millinery: The making of women's hats.

Model millinery: The making of bespoke or limited edition hats.

Parisisal: Woven straw hoods.

Petersham: A grosgrain ribbon.

Pinok pok: High-quality straw, bought by the metre.

Poupee: Another term for dolly head.

Pressing pad: Thick heatproof pad used when ironing.

Right side: The best side of the material.

Self-bind: Binding made of the same material as the hat or headpiece.

Selvedge: The edge of woven material.

Sideband: The side of the crown.

Sinamay: Banana tree fibre.

Sisal: A low-cost type of straw.

Stayflex: A brand of interfacing.

Tarlatan: Non-fusible interfacing.

Thimble: Finger covering to aid sewing and blocking.

Tip: The top of the crown.

Toque: A small hat made from soft fabric, usually without a brim.

Trimming: Decorative details.

Veiling: Open weave or sheer material often draped across the face.

Warp: The vertical weave in a material.

Weft: The horizontal weave in a material.

Wrong side: The reverse of the material.

Suppliers List

Atelier Millinery
Unit 2.16
Second Floor
Kingly Court
London W1B 5PW
Tel: 020 7734 3848
hello@ateliermillinery.com
www.ateliermillinery.com
Many vintage flowers and trimmings. A
good selection of straws and felts.

Barnett Lawson (Trimmings) Ltd
16 Little Portland Street
London W1W 8NE
Tel: 020 7636 8591
info@bltrimmings.com
www.bltrimmings.com
Braids, buttons, sequin motifs,
petersham ribbons, veiling, feathers.
Quills and a variety of feathers by the
metre. Millinery bases and combs.

Baxter Hart & Abraham Ltd
141 New Bedford Road
Luton LU3 1LF
Tel: 01582 721381
HornBHA@aol.com
www.baxterhart.co.uk
Wool felt cones and capeline hoods.
Sinamay, parisisal and many other
straws in current season's colours.
Millinery petersham.

Boon and Lane
7/11 Taylor Street
Luton LU2 0EY
Tel: 01582 723224
www.hatblocks.co.uk
Block-makers to the hat trade (metal and
wood). They will carve wood blocks to
your own design or copy hat shapes.

Guy Morse Brown
2 Snarlton Farm
Snarlton Lane
Melksham
Wiltshire SN12 7QP
01225 899000
mail@hatblocks.co.uk
http://www.hatblocks.co.uk
http://www.hatblocks.com/
Wooden block-maker – order from an
extensive range of starter blocks and
more complicated shapes from a large
catalogue. Multi blocks for new
milliners.

Hat Box Designs
Greywell Press Ltd
42 Invincible Road
Farnborough GU14 7QU
01491 414000
sales@hatboxdesigns.co.uk
www.hatboxdesigns.co.uk

The Hat Magazine
170 Brick Lane
London E1 6RU
Tel: 0207 247 1120
http://www.thehatmagazine.com/
Quarterly Magazine with news of hat
designers and suppliers in Europe, and
trade and hat shop information. Back
issues available.

MacCulloch & Wallis Ltd
25–26 Dering Street
London W1S 1AT
Tel: 020 7629 0311
samples@macculloch.com
www.macculloch-wallis.co.uk
Millinery haberdashers. Straw and felt
stiffening. White/black buckram,
sinamay, petersham ribbons, felt hoods,

straw hoods. Veiling, stayflex, silks,
organza. Large catalogue available.

Martina Bohn Hat Block Hire
07905 375725
www.hatblock.co.uk
enquire@hatblock.co.uk
Wide range of vintage blocks to hire at
very reasonable prices.

Milliner Warehouse
35 Ebury Bridge Road
London SW1W 8QX
Tel: 020 7730 4918
www.millinerwarehouse.com
Big range of sinamay, plain and printed
straw hoods, crin, wool felts, straw
stiffener, felt stiffener, fascinator bases,
mini hats.

Ostrich Feather Manufacturing Co. Ltd
1 Northburgh Street
London EC1V 0AH
Tel: 020 7253 7391
www.ostrichfeather.co.uk
sales@ostrichfeather.co.uk
http://www.ostrichfeather.co.uk/
Big range of fringes, feathers, boas,
marabou, accessories (minimum orders).

Parkin Fabrics Ltd
Prince of Wales Business Park
Vulcan Street
Oldham OL1 4ER
Tel: 0161 627 4455
info@parkinfabrics.co.uk
www.parkinfabrics.co.uk
Fur felt hoods in a good range of
colours. Wool felts, sinamay in seasonal
colours. Crin. Haberdashery and
feathers. Extensive catalogue.

Randalls Ribbons Ltd
12 Frederick Street
Luton LU2 7QS
Tel: 01582 721301
sales@randallsribbons.co.uk
www.randallsribbons.co.uk
Millinery trimmings, sinamay by the roll,
flowers, feathers, straw and fabric,
veiling, ribbons.
Catalogue available.

Rui Tong Trade Ltd
71A Salisbury Street
Hull HU5 3DU
01482 440798
info@ruitongltd.com
www.ruitongltd.com
Feathers, mounts and hat boxes.

The Trimming Company
3 The Workshops
Greenfield Road
Pulloxhill
MK45 5BF
01525 717455
www.thetrimmingcompany.com
Wide range of materials and millinery
accessories. Shop online.

Australia

Melbourne Hat Blocks
Unit 3
2 Celia Street
Bentleigh East
Victoria 3165
+61 (0) 395793434
+61 (0) 411343728
www.melbournehatblocks.com.au

International Millinery Forum
Wagga Wagga City Council Visitor
Information Centre
183 Tarcutta Street
Wagga Wagga
NSW 2650
+611 300 100 122
+612 6926 9621
www.waggawaggaaustralia.com.au

visitors@wagga.nsw.gov.au
Hat event.

Hatters Millinery Supplies
PO Box 7097
Wilberforce
NSW 2756
+61 (0) 245753668
1300 428837
www.hattersmillinerysupplies.com.au
millie@hattersmillinerysupplies.com.au
Millinery supplies.

De Lew Designs
15 Crisp Drive
Wagga Wagga
NSW 2650
+61 (0) 269711122
www.delew.com.au
Dlew8323@bigpond.net.au
Millinery supplies.

Torb and Reiner
101 Poath Road
Murrumbeena 3163
Victoria, Australia
+613 9568 1166
+613 9504 4476
www.torbandreiner.com
info@torbandreiner.com
Millinery supplies.

Belgium

BVBA De Vroey
Ter Rivierenlaan 16
2100 Deurne Antwerp
Belgium
+32 (0) 4 9754 4900
info@devroeyhats.be
www.devroeyhats.be
Millinery supplies.

France

Ets. H. Aschmid
21 Rue d'Uzes 75002
Paris, France
+33 0147426645
Millinery supplies.

Germany

Wolfram Kopka
Am Rankewerk 2–4
D-50321 Bruehl
Germany
+49 02232 42699
info@kopka.de
www.kopka.de
Felt hoods (minimum order).

Heide Steyer
United Röhrsdorfer Str 28
01477 Arnsdorf OT Wallroda
Germany
035 200/23950
www.steyer.eu
Artificial flowers.

Holland

Van Der Broek
Stationsstraat 52
6365 CK Schinnen
The Netherlands
+31 046 443 3899
info@hoedenmallen.nl
www.hoedenmallen.nl

Hoedendingen
Kerkstraat 31
6988 AE Lathum
The Netherlands
+31 (0) 313 632848
info@hoedendingden.nl
www.hoedendingden.nl
Millinery supplies.

H.P. Tex
Staverhul 22a
3888 MR Uddel
The Netherlands
+31 (0) 577 400 730
Hptex@planet.nl
www.Hptex.nl
Millinery suppliers.

Ireland

The Feathered Milliner
34 Wellington Quay
Dublin 2
+ 35316337814
www.thefeatheredmilliner.com

Sunflower Touch Supplier
www.thesunflowertouchsupply.com
brendabergin@yahoo.com

Italy

Fratelli Reali & CSpA
Via Pierluigi da Palestrina 31/33
50144 Firenze

Italy
+30 055 354 655
info@fratellireali.it
www.fratellireali.it
Millinery supplies.

Luigi and Guido Tesi
Via S. Paolo, 149 – 50017 S. Piero a Ponti
(Firenze)
Italy
+39 055 8999019
+39 055 8999595
amministrazione@tesihats.com
www.tesihats.com
http://www.tesihats.com/
Millinery supplies.

Spain

Milliner Warehouse
C/Luchana 16. 1aD
Madrid
28010 Spain
+34 (0) 915229027
spain@millinerwarehouse.com
www.millinerwarehouse.com

USA

Hats by Leko
POB 170 Odell
Oregon 97044
USA
hatsupply@gmail.com
www.hatsupply.com
Millinery supplier.

Judith M
Millinery Supply House
104 South Detroit Street
LaGrange, Indiana 46761
USA
+1 (260) 499 4407
info@judithm.com
www.judithm.com

Further Reference

Design Museum: *Fifty Hats That Changed the World,* Octopus Books
Hopkins, Susie: *The Century of Hats: Headturning Styles of the 20th Century,* Chartwell Books
Jones, Stephen: *Hats: An Anthology,* Victoria & Albert Museum
McDowell, Colin: *Hats: Style, Status and Glamour,* Thames & Hudson Ltd
Papadakis Publishing, *The Hat Book*
Turner Wilcox, R.: *The Mode in Hats and Headdress,* Dover Publications Inc.

Places of Interest

Victoria & Albert Museum, London, UK
Hat Works, Stockport, Lancashire, UK
Wardown Park Museum, Luton, Bedfordshire, UK
The Hat Museum, Portland, Oregon, USA

Featured Milliners

www.ateliermillinery.com
www.bethmorgan.co.uk
www.justinebradley-hills.co.uk
www.karenhenriksen.co.uk
www.lyzehats.co.uk
www.mandymcgregormillinery.co.uk
www.naidarafols.com
www.natashamoorhouse.com
www.rizvimillinery.com
www.sheenaholland.com
www.tracychaplin.co.uk

Index

Related Titles from Crowood

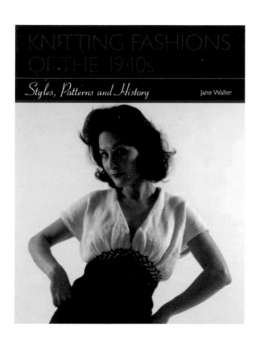

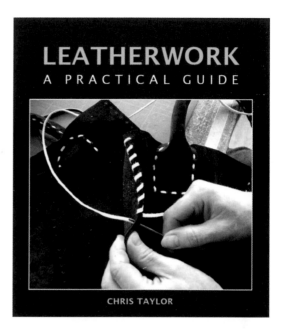

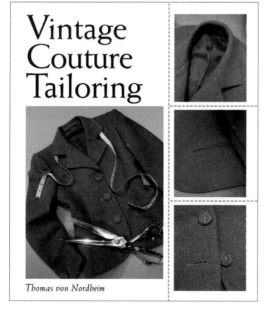

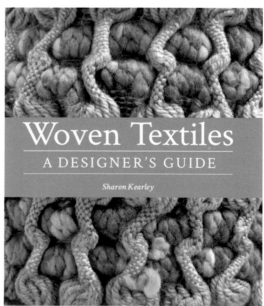